Pre-Classic Dance Forms

by

LOUIS HORST

With a New Foreword by
JANET SOARES
The Juilliard School

D0169259

A DANCE HORIZONS BOOK
Princeton Book Company, Publishers
Princeton, New Jersey

Publisher's Note: *Pre-Classic Dance Forms* was originally published in 1937, and subsequently updated in 1940, 1953, and
1968. It is a classic work in the field of dance history and
choreography. For this reason, we have decided not to make
changes in the original text, except where obvious errors (such
as omitted lines or words) were made in the original typog-
raphy. Readers are encouraged to consult current research
by dance historians and musicologists for further information.

ISBN 916622-51-7

Library of Congress Card Number 74-77180

Printed in the United States of America

A Dance Horizons Book
Princeton Book Company, Publishers
P.O. Box 109
Princeton, NJ 08542

Cover illustration courtesy of Bibliothèque Nationale, Paris, France

Cover design by Design & Illustration

To

Irene Lewisohn,

whose foresight

first made possible new experiments

in these old forms.

Foreword

In 1928, Louis Horst began his search for choreographic trad-
itions that predated ballet. He hoped to find material that
would be applicable to modern dancers who were searching
for new ways to study movement. Nine years later, his studies
bore fruit in the book *Pre-Classic Dance Forms*. Horst continued
to teach this course until his death in 1964. Fifty years after
its first publication, the text remains an important resource
for students, choreographers, stage directors, dance historians, and musicologists.

Horst's ideas on the relationship of dance to the other arts
provided the basis for his enlightened pedagogy. He encouraged musicality, discipline, originality, and respect for histor-
ical dance forms among his students. Horst's special mode of
teaching demonstrated unparalleled results, beginning with
the success of Martha Graham, his "first and best student."

An ardent supporter for modernity in contemporary dance,
Horst believed that dance should no longer be represented
as the handmaiden of music. By returning to a time when
court composers wrote specifically for dance, Horst felt that
a renewed independence could emerge with dance taking a
predominant position. He defined the "pre-classic" period as
one where musical accompaniment provided a framework for
dance, aptly offering a resource for the teaching of formal
principles of composition to dancers.

In 1928, Louis Horst began to teach choreography at the

Neighborhood Playhouse, in the midst of his active career as concert pianist and musical director for the era's most innovative dancers including Agnes de Mille, Doris Humphrey, Michio Ito, Harald Kruetzberg, and Helen Tamiris. For the next six years, Horst researched and experimented with various musical forms. With the precision of an etymologist, he sought definitions from early musicologists, studied the social milieu of distant times and examined the simple structures of rondos, theme and variations, and 2- and 3-part forms. The results of his study were originally published in a series of articles for his journal *Dance Observer* between 1934 and 1937, and were subsequently published in book form in 1937.

Horst lamented the lack of dance literature in an interview in 1936. "We have histories and polemics and panegryics and poetry, but no studies in form and composition. It is very easy for the musician to procure all sorts of theoretical works, but the absence of this same type of material in dance literatures has caused me to use music as form (parallel) examples for [the making of] formal compositions. In a sense, we are returning music to dance from which it originated.*

In *Pre-Classic Dance Forms*, Horst asked students to work with objectivity in a process that required both delineation of movement and the skillful abstraction of ideas—essential goals for potential choreographers. After covering the background of each dance form, he encouraged individual solutions to the formal problems of composition through the creation of a personal movement vocabulary. He effectively used the wide variety of tempos and qualities within the specific forms. This required an intellectual and physical understanding of the

*Gilfond, H., "Louis Horst." *Dance Observer III* (2), February, 1936, p. 4.

musical elements of pulse, meter, phrasing, rhythmic, and dynamic change.

Horst's second course, *Modern Dance Forms,* placed the work of the modern choreographer within the context of the other arts in the 20th century. Louis Horst once commented on his teaching of *Pre-Classic Dance Forms:* "I just took a simple idea." This simple "idea" has introduced generations of choreographers to dance composition. The "pianistic saint of dance," as the newspapers of the 30s called him, Horst taught the formal craft of making dances from his position at the keyboard. His teaching methods are now at the foundation of serious choreographic study throughout the world.

Janet Mansfield Soares

CONTENTS

ILLUSTRATIONS

Introduction

THE secularization of the arts at the time of the Renaissance brought about important changes in music and the dance. Art must serve an ideal, either religion or some consciously held esthetic idea, and during the middle ages the service of western art was for the church. To the Renaissance we owe the transferring of this allegiance from the principles of religion to those of architecture.

In music this change was noticeable both in its tonal and rhythmic aspects. The tonal character of mediaeval music was colored by the exclusive use of the Greek Modes, vividly exemplified in the Gregorian chant. This modal style, coupled with its irregular rhythm, induced the pale and austere mood of monasticism, with which the secular ideals of the opulent Renaissance came into conflict. Secular composers discarded all the modes excepting the Ionian (our major scale) and the Aeolian (from which our minor scale was formed). The Ionian and Aeolian modes had been avoided by the ecclesiastical composers, on account of "their wordly association and irreligious characters," one writer, Glareanus, stating that "these two modes are particularly adapted to dances"; another mentions the sweetness of the Ionian compared with the more archaic modes; still another illustrates the depravity of his age with the declaration that "marriageable young women delight in learning Ionian dances."

The rhythmic change was equally important. Although the Gregorian chant adopted the Greek Modes, via the bridge of

[1]

Byzantine art, it did not retain the strong rhythmic quality of Greek music. We are very ignorant of Greek music, but we know its purpose was to serve the uses of poetry; hence we are able to presuppose its primarily metric structure. On the contrary, the Gregorian chant applied these modes to the irregular rhythms of Latin prose. And with this subtle irregularity of rhythm the architecturally-minded Renaissance also came into conflict. There developed a definite trend to monody (i.e., a single melodic line with a definite rhythmic accompaniment); a perpendicular, or harmonic concept of music, instead of the linear or horizontal style of the mediaevalists. For this *new* harmonic style it was inevitable that the composers should select the Ionian mode; for, "it is harmonic in feeling, and indissolubly bound up with the harmonic series" (of over-tones), "whereas the other old modes are wholly melodic in feeling, and hostile to harmony." (Cecil Gray)

A consideration of these two important changes in music must prove that the development of a period of great dance music was inevitable, or rather, when, in the fifteenth and sixteenth centuries, a great dance movement swept over cultural Europe, music was prepared to serve it. It has been for this reason that these aspects of musical change have been dwelt upon.

It may be true that a great period in architecture always goes hand in hand with a like period in the dance, but the dance of the Italian Renaissance proved at first anything but great and had to wait until transported to France for its full and formalized development into a great art. It was the union of the lighter, though patrician art of the south with the more vigorous, though sometimes plebeian art of the north, that brought forth this new social rite, known as the court

[2]

(*Charbonnel. La Danse.*)

BRANLE

dance. It was a blend of the rich brilliance of Italian life, the sombre, religious emotion of Spanish life, the rude intellectual vitality of the Netherlands, and the pastoral serenity of English ideals. To this must be added the influence of the popular art of the Troubadours and their Courts of Love in France, and the dance-tune hymns of Martin Luther's Reformation in Germany.

Other external but important influences must be mentioned; the invention of printing, together with great improvements in the calligraphy of music and the birth of dance script. Their dissemination among the laity encouraged the recording and preserving of the contemporary art forms. Hitherto the sole repositories for learning had been the monasteries, and the monks could hardly be expected to keep records of such profane arts as the dance and its accompanying music. Strangely enough, however, the first, and still probably the finest history of the dances of his time, was written in 1588 by a monk named Jehan Tabourot. It is called *Orchesographie,* and was written under the pseudonym of Thoinot Arbeau. No study of these dance forms can even be attempted without a perusal of this work.

Another external event of importance was the transplanting of Catherine de Medici and her luxury-loving court from Italy to France. These facts, and more could be cited, only go to prove that if we owe the renaissance of dancing to Italy, we owe its development to France. Up to this time dances had only general classifications. The *Branle* was susceptible to a variety of forms—some in 4/4 time, others in 3/4 or 2/4. There were the *Branle de Poitou, Branle des Brandons, Branle mimes,* etc. There was the *basse danse* in which the feet did not leave the floor, also the *haute danse* in which there

[4]

were skips and jumps, but still no prescribed forms. During the sixteenth century we see great results in clarification, and rules were formulated for the proper steps for each dance, and the proper strict form for the music thereto. Here we have the greatest benefit this period bestowed. On the side of the dance, we see evolving from it a new ballet with form, rules and a vocabulary of steps. Musically, the different dance forms through the need for contrast soon were grouped into a certain order by the composers, giving birth to the Suite. Couperin called his Suites *Ordres*. And it was this same Suite which served as a cradle from which was reared the most important form of the entire classic period, the Sonata form.

It is not necessary for one to agree with the artistic taste displayed to realize that this was indeed an important period for the dance. It was a time when almost all the great music was dance music. Modern composers, in their return to architectural principles after the bathos of romanticism, again are writing Pavanes, Sarabandes, Passepieds, Gavottes, etc. These include such names as Satie, Fauré, Debussy, Ravel, Prokofieff, Honegger and Schoenberg. True, they are of modern harmonic texture, and of larger dimension, no longer the rather trite two-part form of the originals, but considering the evolution of music and thought since the sixteenth century, they could not be otherwise.

Of the dance we must admit that it truthfully reflected the life of that period, even though it may seem baroque, and later decidedly rococo, to us. But of the two, music has fared better than the dance, primarily because we do not demand of music that it always reflect our age, whereas its contemporaneousness with the tempo of our time is the gauge by which we measure the dance.

[5]

PAVANE
at the Court of Louis XIII

Pavane

Who doth not see the measures of the Moone,
Which thirteene times she daunceth every year?
And ends her *Pavine* thirteene times as soone
As doth her brother.

(Sir John Davies,—*Orchestra,* 1596).

THE ceremonious dignity, splendor and grave pride inherent in the steps and music of the Pavane are suggested by its name, which is derived from the Latin —*Pavo*—*peacock.* The dance brings to one's mind all the metaphors suggestive of that stately and pompous fowl. Its origin can be traced to the formal and austere court life of inquisitional Spain, and therefore we must inevitably add to its characteristics that of a sombre religious mood. This close relationship to the church gave the music much of its chant-like quality.

Dancing always had been an integral part of the ceremony in the churches of Spain on notable occasions. The well known *Pavane for a Defunct Infanta* by Ravel (1875—) was undoubtedly suggested by this fact. The Pavane *Saint Thomas Wake,* by John Bull (1563-1628), likewise suggests a religious conception. Our great authority Arbeau (b. 1519), in his *Orchesographie* (1588), informs us that "our musicians play it when a damsel of good family is taken to Holy Church to be married, or when musicians head a religious procession of the chaplains, masters, and brethren of some notable guild."

[7]

Some authorities hold that the Spanish Pavane was a variation of the original dance, which had an Italian origin, and view *Pavana* as reduced from *Padovana* (*Paduan*). But the Oxford Dictionary claims the phonetic difficulties in identifying the two words are serious, and that they are probably distinct terms, which may afterwards have been confused by those who knew the history of one of them only. Also, according to the Dictionary of the Spanish Academy, *Pavana* (found in the *Diccionario Pisado,* 1552) is a derivative of *"Pavo-peacock."* The old German name was *Pfauentanz-peacock dance.* The weight of testimony certainly seems to favor a Spanish origin.

The Pavane sustained its popularity from about 1530 to 1676. One of the earliest allusions to the Pavane in English literature was written in 1530 by Elyot: "We have nowe base daunsis, pavions, turgions, and roundes." This is affirmed by Lyndesay, another writer of the sixteenth century, who in 1535 wrote:

> "We sall leir now to dance
> Ane new Pavin of France."

At the Spanish and French courts the Pavane was developed into a processional pageant of great dignity and an imposing spectacle. It was one of the oldest *Basse Danses,* (literally, low dance, or a dance in which the feet of the performers did not leave the floor.) Dances which required jumping were called *Haute Danses.* The *Dictionnaire de Trevoux* (1721) describes the Pavane as a "grave kind of dance, borrowed from the Spaniards, wherein the performers make a kind of a wheel or tail before each other, like that of a peacock, whence the name." It achieved the title of *Le Grand*

Bal, and usually constituted the opening of all ceremonious balls, generally being followed by the livelier Galliard. "It is used by kings, princes and great lords, to display themselves on some day of solemn festival with their fine mantles and robes of ceremony; and then the queens and princesses and the great ladies accompany them with the long trains of their dresses let down and trailing behind them. These Pavanes are also used in masquerades (or ballets) when there is a procession of triumphal chariots of gods and godesses, emperors or kings resplendent with majesty" (Arbeau). The spirit of such a scene is caught in the following verse:

> Splendour dorée et rose et bleue
> D'un innombrable diamant
> Le paon miraculeusement
> Developpers son ample queue;
> En la largeur de ses deplis
> Tout un etal d'orfèvre tremble,
> Et la Pavane lui ressemble
> Mais aver des pied plus jolis!

It was a grand, a solemn, and a majestic dance, often accompanied by a song, with hautboys, while drums accented the rhythm. This drum rhythm is clearly illustrated in the Pavane *Belle Qui Tiens Ma Vie* from Arbeau's *Orchesographie*. Additional evidence of the high esteem in which it was held can be gathered from an old engraving showing the Cardinals of Narbonne and Saint Severin dancing a Pavane before Louis XII, at Milan, in 1499. Chambonnieres (1620-1670) composed a Pavane with the high-sounding title of *L'Entretien des Dieux.*

That the Pavane never became much more than a simple walking, with slight variations, is self-evident; the chief

BELLE QUI TIENS MA VIE

(PAVANE)

Tirée de l'Orchesographie de **JEAN TABOURET** (1589)

Cette pavane est un modèle des danses chantées au temps de la Renaissance. Écrite pour les quatre voix du quatuor mixte, on la peut toutefois chanter à voix seule, les autres parties servant d'accompagnement instrumental.

C'est là une danse noble, une danse de cour dont on ne saurait trop marquer les cérémonieuses cadences. On ne doit point négliger la partie de tambour (ou tambourin qui rythme et précise le pas).

Nous devons ces trois monuments d'un archaïsme si expressif à la complaisance éclairée de M. Henry Expert, l'organisateur averti des Concerts historiques du samedi à l'Opéra-Comique, où ils vont être chantés.

Viens tôt me se _ cou _ rir   Ou   me   fau _ dra   mou _ rir,

Viens tôt me se _ cou _ rir   Ou   me   fau _ dra   mou _ rir.

II	IV	VI

Pourquoy fuis tu, mignarde,
Si je suis pres de toy?
Quand tes yeulx je regarde,
Je me perds dedans moy,
Car tes perfections
Changent mes actions.

Mon âme vouloit estre
Libre de passions,
Mais amour s'est faict maistre
De mes affections,
Et a mis soubs sa loy
Et mon cœur et ma foy

Je meurs, mon Angelette,
Je meurs en te baisant;
Ta bouche tant doucette
Va mon bien ravissant,
A ce coup mes espritz
Sont tous d'amour espris.

III	V	VII

Tes beautez et ta grace
Et tes divins propos
Ont eschauffé la glace
Qui me geloit les os
Et ont remply mon cœur
D'une amoureuse ardeur

Approche donc, ma belle,
Approche toy, mon bien.
Ne me sois plus rebelle,
Puis que mon cœur est tien,
Pour mon mal appaiser
Donne moy un baiser.

Plustost on verra l'onde
Contre mont reculer,
Et plustost l'œil du monde
Cessera de brusler,
Que l'amour qui m'époinct
Decroisse d'un seul poinct.

dictum required that "the students of this dance must enshroud their very souls with majestic dignity." It was danced in a slow tempo, by one couple or many couples. Before beginning the dance the performers walked gravely around the room and saluted the King and Queen, or the great dignitaries who gave the ball. The steps were simple and were called *advancing* and *retreating*. In *retreating*, the gentlemen walked behind their ladies, leading them by the hand; a few gliding steps and a great many curtseys followed, and everyone regained his place. Next, one of the gentlemen advanced alone, and, describing a slight curve in the middle of the ballroom, went *en se pavanant* (strutting like a peacock) to salute the lady opposite him. Finally, taking some backward steps, he regained his place, bowing to his own lady. The above description of the figures illustrates the simplicity of the Pavane.

About 1857, during his travels in Spain, Baron Davillier (1823-1883) found the following colloquial uses of the word *Pavane* still in vogue. "To this day in Spain, they speak of *son entrados de Pavana*—the Pavane-like entry of a man who comes mysteriously and with ponderous gravity to say something ridiculously unimportant." And also, *"son pasos de Pavana* is said of a personage whose walk is affectedly slow." He quoted a Spanish author as saying: "The Pavana mimics the charming attitudes of the regal peacock, who sways about as if he were on wheels."

Shakespeare refers to the Pavane in a rather cryptic fashion in *Twelfth Night*:

> "Then he's a rogue, and a passy measures pavyn;
> I hate a drunken rogue."

This obscure passage has caused much questioning by Shakespearian annotators. It seems best answered by one who discovered a manuscript of a *passinge measure Pavyon** containing the following directions for dancing it:

> Two singles and a double forward, and two singles syde.
> Reprynce (repeat?) back.

The form of the music, like the steps, is simple; a very slow 4/4 or 2/2 rhythm, beginning solidly on *one,* and containing no florid or running passages. A Pavane consisted of two or three strains of eight, twelve or sixteen bars each. We can gain no better understanding of the music than by conning the pages of the musicologists of the period. Butler, in *Principles of Music* (1636), speaking of the Doric mode, has the following: "Of this sort are Pavins, invented for a slow and soft kind of dancing, altogether in duple (2/2) proportion." Thomas Morley, in *A Plaine and Easie Introduction to Practical Musicke* (1597), says, "The next in gravity and goodness is called a Pavane, a kind of steide musicke, ordained for grave dauncing. In this you must cast you musicke by foures (4/4). After every Pavane we usually set a Galliard." With this coupling of the Pavane and the Galliard (a slow 4/4 or 2/2 followed by a quick 3/4) the all-important Suite was born, or, at least, its forerunner.

According to Parry, the eminent contemporary English musicologist, the English composers appear to have illustrated the manner of transition from the individual dance forms to Suites much more clearly than the composers of other countries. The Pavane appears so frequently at the beginning of a Suite that it is scarcely to be doubted that composers actually regarded it as the most eligible preliminary movement,

---

* *Passy Measures* is a corruption of Passamezzo—an Italian variant of the Pavane. See *Lesser Forms.*

just as the courts had regarded it for their balls. It was generally written in a very solid style, and with such contrapuntal devices as completely obscured its dance origin. Thus it became a massive prelude from which developed the introductory measures to the overtures of the classic period, known to musicians as the "French Overture." Later (about 1620) the Allemande supplanted the Pavane as the initial movement of instrumental Suites. This will be discussed fully in the chapter dealing with the Allemande.

Among the best known of these forerunners of the Suite, we must mention John Dowland's *Lachrymae, or Seven Teares, figured in Seven Passionate Pavans* (1605). Two of the oldest and finest Pavanes recorded are those quoted by Arbeau; the lovely song *Belle Qui Tiens Ma Vie,* and a *Pavane d'Espagne.* Others famous in their time are *The Earle Of Salisbury Pavan,* by William Byrde (1538-1623), and *Nopce de Village,* by Lully (1633-1687).

Although greatly indebted to the form, the composers of the classic and romantic periods wrote no openly avowed Pavanes, until Gabriel Faure (1845-1924) produced, in 1901, the *Pavane for Chorus and Orchestra, Opus 50.* Since then many other modern musicians have often turned to these earlier forms for inspiration. The old dance forms have had a rebirth; and of modern Pavanes we have many excellent examples. Among the outstanding ones are those of Bainton, Messager, Merigot, Albeniz, Poulenc, and the two well-known ones by Ravel, the aforementioned *Pavane pour une Infante Defunte,* and the *Pavane de La Belle au Bois Dormant,* the first number of his *Mother Goose* Suite.

These old forms can serve the dancer as well as the musician. The pulse and form of the Pavane combine to make an ideal

[14]

ANGNA ENTERS
in Pavana, Spain, 16th Century.

accompaniment for any dance, subjective or objective, in which the mood desired is one of power, slow-moving strength, or extreme formality. The slow tempo of the music and the extreme gravity of the steps have also rendered this dance useful as a means of ridiculing eccentricities. Of the more objective examples among modern dancers we must mention Angna Enters' splendid *Pavana, Spain, 16th century,* in which she has brought out all the ominous Borgia-like spirit of Spain of that period. An excellent abstract example is the highly formalized group dance, *Masque,* the second movement of Martha Graham's Suite *Chronicle,* to which Wallingford Riegger has composed the music. On a recent tour the Jooss Ballet presented a stylized, though more obviously theatrical group dance, entitled *Pavane for a Dead Infanta,* to Ravel's music.

GALLIARD

(Arbeau. Orchesographie.)

Galliard

Capriol—Well, here I am, holding a
          damsel by the hand; my
          reverence is made, my bonnet
          replaced, and my features
          composed. In what manner
          shall I begin?
              (Arbeau: *Orchesographie* 1588).

FOR any information regarding the Galliard (*Fr*: gaillarde; *It*: gagliarda) we can go to no more complete
source than did *Capriol,* when he desired to learn the steps of
this dance. For Arbeau has written at greater length of the
Galliard than has any other author, and also more of the
Galliard than he has of any other dance. In his unique
Orchesographie (Beaumont translation) there are fully forty
pages devoted to it; the steps of at least twenty Galliards are
given, as well as the melodic phrases of many popular Galliard tunes of that day.

Arbeau says, "The Galliard is so called because one must
be blithe and lively to dance it." Another definition, directly
from the dictionary, has *galliard*—a gay or dashing person
(from the old French: *galach-lively*). "Come, Madam, let's
be frolick, galliard, and extraordinary brisk." (Shadwell,
1671.) These fully explain the outstanding characteristic of
the dance: that of gaiety. But it is a vigorous, a strong gaiety.
In the Oxford Dictionary we find an obsolete use of the ad-

jective *galliard*. There it is defined as *hardy, valiant, sturdy*. In 1533 Elyot writes, "Vehement exercise is compounde of violent exercise and swifte when they ar joyned togither at one tyme, as dansyng of galyardes."

The origin of the Galliard is attributed to Italy, where it was also known as the Romanesca, and according to some Italian authorities its name was derived from *gigolane*, namely *kicking*. It enjoyed its greatest period of popularity from the last quarter of the sixteenth century to the middle of the seventeenth century. Shakespeare refers to it often, especially in *Twelfth Night*:

"Why dost thou not go to church in a galliard and come home in a coranto?"
"I did think, by the excellent constitution of thy leg, it was formed under the star of a galliard."

and in *King Henry the Fifth*:

"—the prince our master
Says that you savour too much of your youth
And bids you be advised
There's nought in France
That can be with a nimble galliard won."

Indeed, the fact has come down to us from the pen of Parnakh in his *Histoire de la Danse* that Elizabeth of England exercised each morning by doing six or seven Galliards.

Arbeau tells us that "it is usual for the Pavane to be succeeded by the Gaillarde." When it became customary to follow the slow stately Pavane in 4/4 time with the quicker and gay Galliard in 3/4 time, for sake of contrast, the Suite was born. That was really an important event, especially when we follow further the development of this dance Suite into the Sonata form of the classic music era. In many cases the Gal-

Queen Elizabeth dancing *lavolta* with the Earl of Leicester.

liard was constructed from the same melodic theme as the Pavane which preceded it. And Thomas Morley (1597) insists upon the following rhythmic unity: "How manie foures of semibreves you put in the straine of your pavan, so many times sixe minimes must you put in the straine of your galliard." The Pavane and Galliard by Phalese (1571) and the Paduan and Galliard by Peuerl (1575-1625), both in *Geschichte der Musik in Beispielen,* (published in 1931 by Breitkopf and Härtel) are excellent examples of this embryonic Suite in only two parts.

However, the oldest form of the Galliard was called the Tourdion, and was, as Arbeau says, "danced more quietly and with less violent actions." There were really three varieties of the Galliard. The Tourdion, for the more stately dancers, was danced with gliding steps, the feet not leaving the floor. The Galliard itself, for the less stately, was danced with many kicks, hops, and jumps. Barnabe Riche (1581) has left us his impressions of this variety: "Our small galliardes are so curious, thei are not for my daunsying, for thei are so full of trickes and tournes, that he which hath no more but the plain sinque pace is not better accoumpted of than a verie bongler."

One authority tells us that in the Tourdion the lady was always led by the hand, whereas in the Galliard everyone danced alone. The Tourdion was an opportunity for the more skillful dancers, first the lady dancing alone, then the gentleman. Arbeau counsels *Capriol* to be "modest"—"that is to say, to dance close to the ground, to make the five steps quietly, and further, to make a circle round the room, holding your damsel the while. Then, taking your *congé* when you are so inclined, you will let her dance alone, and beginning to dance your five steps higher from the ground until you return

[21]

in front of her. Then in lively spirits, you will make such passages as please you. For, if you spring too gaily at the beginning, it would seem as if you wish to perform impossibilities."

The third variety is known as the Volté, popular with the young and agile dancers because of the turning and lifting of the girls by their partners. Arbeau suggests the vigor of the Volté and its departure from the usual refinement and grace. "After having turned for as many cadences as it pleases you, restore the damsel to her place, when she will feel, whatever good face she puts upon it, her brain confused, her head full of giddy whirlings, and you cannot feel in much better case. I leave you to consider if it be a proper thing for a young girl to make such large steps and separations of the legs; and whether both honour and health are not concerned and threatened." In spite of his moral concern, Arbeau on the very next page gives *Capriol* the following sound and lusty directions: "If you wish to dance the Volté, you should place your right hand on the damsel's back and the left below her bust, and, pushing her with your right thigh beneath her rump, turn her." This lack of refinement may have been the reason for Praetorious' (b. 1571) declaiming against the Galliard; calling it "an invention of the devil, full of shameful and obscene gestures and immodest movements." After the foregoing descriptions it is not surprising that the ladies of the period ornamented their garters with their most precious laces of gold and silver. What is surprising is that Desrat (in *Traite de la Danse*) states that "it was unknown to the common people, as the gaillarde was always reserved for the gentlewomen and the gentlemen." During the reign of the chaste Louis XIII, the Volté disappeared completely. The Galliard

[22]

GAGLIARDA

Hans Leo Hassler. (1564-1612)

followed soon after as we do not find it under Louis XIV.

All three varieties of the Galliard were based on its outstanding rhythmic characteristic, that which gave it its other name of *Cinque Pas* (*Five Steps*), or, as we find it in old English plays, *Cincopace*. As Arbeau explains it, "the Galliard ought to consist of six steps, seeing that it contains six crotchets (quarter-notes) played in two bars of triple (3/4) time. All the same there are only five steps, because the fifth and penultimate note is lost in the air." On the count of *five* the dancers always executed either a little or a big jump, landing in a cadent posture on the count of *six*. In the Tourdion the jump was little, in the Galliard the jump was big, and in the Volté the man lifted his partner on this count of *five*. In England, during that time, the jump or leap on the count of *five* was known as the *caper*. To quote again from *Twelfth Night*: when Sir Toby asks, "What is thy excellence in a Galliard, knight?", Sir Andrew answers, "I can cut a caper."

In the early musical settings we very often find no note on the count of *five*. *God Save the King* (undoubtedly an old Galliard tune) is a fine example, if not one of the gayest.

Exceptionally fine Galliards were written by Hassler, Frescobaldi, Peuerl, Byrde and Dowland. The writer has discovered no modern examples, although Respighi (1879-1936) transcribed one by Galilei (1550), which is rather full, but not very modern in texture. The modern dancers have likewise neglected this form. Students, however, should still find it an excellent pulse for a dance of sturdy, strong, and gay movement. And a good kinesthetic hint for a subjective or abstract approach is to be found in Funk and Wagnall's Dictionary which defines *gay* as derived from the old French, *gahi,* meaning *quick and sudden.*

Allemande

THE earliest English reference to the Allemande is found in a Scotch chronicle of 1549: "Thai dancit al cristyn mennis dance, the alman haye." However, as indicated by its name, the Allemande (in Old English, *alman, almain* or *almayne*) has an allemanic or German ancestry, and it is the only form contributed to this galaxy of courtly dances by the Germans. It was a very old mediaeval dance, and, in its primitive form, was undoubtedly performed with no great grace. For example, Peele, in 1584, refers to "Knights in armour, treading a warlike almain." In 1597 Thomas Morley described it as "a more heavy daunce, fitlie representing the nature of the people whose name it carrieth, so that no extraordinary motions are used in the dauncing of it." Arbeau also does not accord it much style, and calls it a "plain dance of a certain gravity, . . . with little variety of movement."

After being introduced at the court of France it rapidly took on the extremely graceful and sentimental characteristics that procured for it great popularity and the rather paradoxical name of *allemande francaise.* Half a century after Morley's description we have another English musician defining *allmaines* as "lessons, very ayrey and lively" (Thomas Mace, *Musick's Monument,* 1650). This resembles the spirit given us by Arbeau in his account of the dance: "In dancing the

[25]

ALLEMANDE

(12 Figures)

(S. Guillaume. Positions et attitudes de l'Allemande.)

Allemande, a young man may sometimes steal a damsel, taking her from her partner; and the one who is thus robbed endeavours to capture another's. But I do not approve at all of this manner of dancing it, since it may lead to quarrels and discontent."

But the bulk of testimony, and the music that has come down to us, do not give evidence of any accent upon airy liveliness. On the contrary, the beauty of the Allemande lay in its rather slow and flowing grace, especially of the arms, and in its outstanding peculiarity that required the partners' hands remaining joined throughout all the "turns and evolutions of the dance." Praetorious (in *Syntagma musicum,* 1619) writes: *"Allemande* means this much, as a little German song or dance, because *Alemagna* means *Germania* and *un Alemand, a German*. But this dance is not so dexterous and agile as the Galliard, but on the contrary somewhat melancholy and slower." In giving up its earlier heritage of German heaviness, it had acquired the more appealing characteristics of sentiment and tenderness.

As the outstanding trait of the German people is sentiment, it was logical that the Allemande should have become the most sentimental of all court dances. And, as Delsarte claims, if the most sentimental part of the body is the inside of the arm, it is again logical that the Allemande should be the only court dance in which the dancer held both of his or her partner's hands. Long after the Allemande had ceased to exist as a dance, it was remembered as a step. To *Allemande* meant to turn one's partner with arms interlaced.

In Desrat's *Dictionnaire de la Danse* there is a rather full-blown eulogy of the Allemande by Dorat, a poet of the period. A literal translation follows:

[28]

La Declamation

"Happy Germany is simple in its dance.
She has given to us one, which, in our fetes,
To our young beauties, renders many conquests.
Learn all of these steps, all these enchainings,
These natural gestures so full of sentiment;
This amorous labyrinth; this mobile bower,
Where arms cling in crossing and circling;
And this snare so sweet, where the tender enchaining
Permits a theft which is so often forbidden."

This, (despite the hyperbolical images,) together with the accompanying eighteenth century print, leaves little more to be said of the dance.

As to the musical form, we find that it consists of the usual two sections (very often of an uneven number of measures) in four–quarter time, usually beginning with a short eighth or sixteenth note up-beat. The tempo is rather slow and dignified, but gives a sense of flowing movement through the use of many sixteenth notes in its melodic structure. It is simple and straightforward. Mattheson (*The Complete Conductor,* 1739) defines it as "a broken,* serious, and well-elaborated composition, which bears the image of a contented or happy mind that delights in good order and repose. As a truly German invention, it precedes the Courante, just as this precedes the Sarabande and Gigue; which sequence of melodies one calls by the name of Suite."

The Allemande's chief claim to distinction might be said to rest upon its supplanting the Pavane as the opening movement of the great Suites of the classic period. Moser (*Musik Lexikon*) places the date of this change about 1620. Yet

---

* *Broken* refers to the broken-chord element, used to bring about rhythmic flow.

ALLEMANDE

G. F. Handel. (1685-1759)

fifty years later we find "To play first a grave pavin *or* almain" (Shadwell, 1676.) The English evidently did not accept this change as readily as the Germans.

But the change was inevitable, and was due to at least two causes. The primary one, obviously, was the ascendency of the German composers in the world of music at that time. It is easy to understand why these composers, with nationalistic fervor, should wish to commence their Suites with the Allemande. The second and more legitimate reason, was probably due to the outstanding, and diametrically opposed, qualities of the two forms. Though both in a slow 4/4 pulse, the hard and inflexible quality of the Pavane did not prove nearly as structurally pliant a medium for musical manipulation as the softer and more plastic melodic line of the Allemande. In attaining this stature as an important instrumental piece, it probably underwent a greater change than any of the other dance forms. Ernst Mohr has traced this long development in an excellent analytical work entitled *Die Allemande; eine Untersuchung ihrer Entwicklung von den Anfängen bis zu Bach und Händel.* (Hug & Co. Leipzig, 1932.) An English musicologist, Dr. Frederick Niecks, has also written two splendid articles on *The Allemande in the Suite.* They appear in the *London Monthly Musical Record* (Vol. 40, Nos. 472-473, 1910.)

Musical history records many fine Allemandes. We find the oldest that have come down to us in the book by Ernst Mohr. He quotes the first *latinized* one encountered; a short eight-measure Almande by Peter Phalese, published at Lyons in 1546. Then, in order, he gives us seven Allemaignes by Tielman Susato, Antwerp, 1551; four Allemandes by Claude Gervaise, from *Troisieme livres de danceries, Paris,* 1556, and nine more Almandes by Phalese, published in 1571 at Antwerp. One cannot help but notice the close resemblance of these Allemandes to the Pavane; no up-beat, no flowing passages of sixteenth notes, and even very few eighth notes.

Outstanding Allemandes of the later period are those by Purcell, Blow, Bach, Handel, and Francois Couperin. Couperin always titled the Allemandes of his Suites, which he called *Ordres*. Some of these are *La Superbe, La Regente, La Misterieuse, La Castelane, L'audaceuse,* and even *La Couperin*. The finest of them, however, is the dramatic *La Tenebreuse (The Dark One.)*

Modern composers have not turned to the Allemande as they have to the other pre-classic forms, probably because of its essential character of sentimentality; a mood that has been approached with great caution by the composer as well as the dancer of today. The very nature of its flowing phrases is in direct opposition to the shorter, sharper and more ecomical phrase-construction of our time. This has not been true of the Pavane or Sarabande, as their simple construction and depth of emotion, rather than sweet sentiment, have appealed directly to the modern composer. The only Allemandes written by contemporary composers, and known to the writer, are those of Niemann and Prokofieff. Dance students should however still find this form useful for experiments with arm movements, and the projection of sentiment *sans* sentimentality.

(Lambranzi. New School of Theatrical Dancing)

COURANTE

Courante

"The voltés, courantes, and vyolent daunses proceed from furie."

(Sir E. Hoby, 1586.)

THE Courante was a great favorite for two centuries (about 1550 to 1750), and passed through three distinct developments during its long existence. No other court dance sustained its popularity for such a long period, with the possible exception of the Minuet. Indeed, for some time the rivalry between the teachers of these two dances was extremely bitter.

Concerning its origin, we find a great difference of opinion. Some authorities attribute it to Italy, while others say it originated in the French province of Poitou. Both claims, however, are probably correct, the Courante really stemming from two separate sources.

The first form of the Courante, called the Corrente (from the Latin: *curro—to run*), undoubtedly came from Italy. It answered truly to its etymological meaning, the music consisting chiefly of running passages of eighth notes in a rapid ¾ time. It was one of the dances brought over from Italy to France by Catherine de Medici. The period of this type of Courante is set by the above quotation from Sir Hoby, (1586) and by the following lines from Sir John Davies' *Orchestra,*

[34]

(1596), probably the finest of the early works on dancing written in English.

> "What shall I name those current travases,
> That on a triple dactyl foot do run
> Close to the ground with sliding passages,
> Wherein that dancer greatest praise hath won,
> Which with best order can all order shun:
> For everywhere he wantonly must range,
> And turn and wind with unexpected change."

A year later, in 1597, Thomas Morley describes "the Volté rising and leaping, the Courante travising and running." (*A Plaine and Easie Introduction to Practical Musicke.*) In Germany it was known as *Spring Tanz.* Fonta informs us that "it is danced with short passages of *coming and going,* and has a very pliant movement of the knees, which recalls that of a fish when it plunges lightly through the water and returns suddenly to the surface." (*Introduction to the French edition of Arbeau*). Among the Courantes of this classification we find many excellent ones by Lully, Zipoli, Blow, Kirnberger and Loeillet.

The second form, which undoubtedly had its origin in France, is the true court dance form, to which the Courante owed its long and great popularity. Known as the *Branle of Poitou,* it is one of the oldest figure dances that has been handed down to us. Originally it seems to have been a pantomime dance in double rhythm. The following is Arbeau's description of such a Courante:

"In my young days there was a kind of game and ballet arranged to the Courante. For three young men would choose three girls, and having placed themselves in a row, the first dancer would lead his damsel to the end of the room, when

[35]

ALLEGRO

CORRENTE

J. P. Kirnberger. (1721-1783)

MODERATO.

COURANTE. (6/4-3/2 Variety)

J. C. de Chambonnieres. (1620-1670)

he would return alone to his companions. The second would do the same, then the third, so that the three girls were left by themselves at one end of the room and three young men at the other. And when the third had returned, the first, gambolling and making all manner of amorous glances, pulling his hose tight and setting his shirt straight, went to claim his damsel, who refused his arm and turned her back upon him; then, seeing the young man had returned to his place, she pretended to be in despair. The two others did the same. At last all three went together to claim their respective damsels, and kneeling on the ground, begged this boon with clasped hands, when the damsels fell into their arms and all danced the Courante pell-mell." (*Orchesographie*, 1588.)

With this description Arbeau quotes four bars of music for a Courante, in 2/2 time. This duple rhythm must have been transformed into 3/4 (or 3/2) time long before the Courante had won its success at court, as we find none by the great composers other than in triple rhythm. In contrast to the early Courantes which Thomas Macy (1650) describes as "full of sprightliness and vigour," this type is not in rapid tempo and there are fewer iively passages of eighth notes. In fact, the tempo is moderately grave and more often in 3/2 time than in 3/4. This form of the Courante was even considered by d'Alembert as a *slow* Sarabande, while the famous dancing master, Pécour, taught it not unlike the Minuet. Charbonnel (in *La Danse*) adds that it was above all a dance of attitudes, and, at one time, owing to its gravity, was called *La Danse de Docteurs*. However, despite all its air of nobility, by which the lords showed off their grand manners and their gallantry with all frankness, it still contained some running and gliding, and steps done with a slight jump; these steps often describing a zigzag pattern across the floor.

This is the type of Courante which caused Johann Mattheson (*Der Vollkommene Capellmeister,* 1739) quite a sentimental brain-storm. The usually logical German composer and musicologist says: "If the Courante is to be danced, we find this unalterable rule, of which the composer must take particular care, whether he has conceived it as from the orchestra, from the Low German, etc. No time-measure other than the 3/2 is permitted therein."

"It attains its name through a continuous running; it is wholly justified in doing so; yet it must occur charmingly and tenderly."

"The masterpiece of the lutenists, especially in France, is generally the Courante, upon which one can employ his efforts and skill to good purpose. The passion or emotion that should be brought out in a Courante is that of sweet hope. For we find in this melody something courageous, something desirous, and also something delightful: all of them parts of which hope is composed."

He then goes on to defend his sentimental interpretation: "As no person may yet have said this, or seriously have thought on, so many will believe I sought in these matters that which was not to be found, but had its birth in my own brain. But I can lay before every one's eyes the palpable evidence of these above-mentioned three conditions from which follows the existing emotion, which is to be found, and must be, in every good Courante. I am absolutely certain, if the lovers of the lute will examine their Courantes, they will discover this to be equally true."

BERTA OCHSNER
in The King Points Out the Fine Points of the Courante

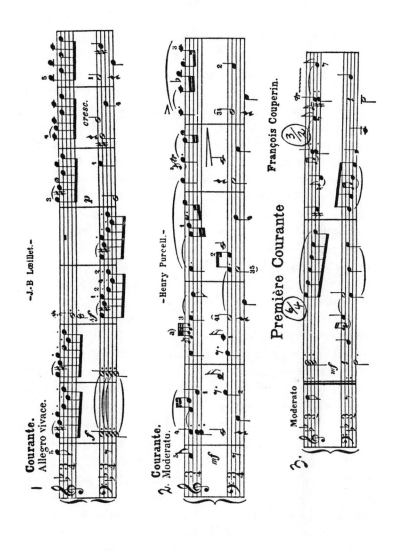

According to Mattheson, hope must be springing eternal in the human breast to a Courante rhythm.

The third classification, known as the instrumental form of Courante, was evolved from the former two by the musicians of the period. They made one measure of 6/4 time out of two measures of 3/4, and, using the number six as the least common multiple, produced effective changes of rhythm by writing some measures in 6/4 time (2 times 3 with the pulse on 1 and 4), and some in 3/2 time (3 times 2 with the pulse on 1, 3 and 5). There was no rule as to when these changes should occur. In fact, each of these Courantes seems to have a different rhythmic scheme. We find, however, that the last measure is always in 6/4 time, and the penultimate measure almost always in 3/2 time. No description of the steps of the Courante ever gives any hint as to the necessity for this change of rhythm, so that we infer it was probably a device originated by the composers. Francois Couperin was the most prolific composer of the Courantes in this classification, although Bach, Chambonnieres and Rameau have also contributed some fine examples. Berta Ochsner has used these changes of rhythm very effectively in a dance entitled *The King Points Out the Fine Points of the Courante,* to Chambonnieres' music.

The accompanying illustration shows a few opening measures of the three different types. The first, by Loeillet, is a good example of the Italian running Corrente; the second, by Purcell, is the stately court Courante in a moderate tempo; the third, by Couperin, is the instrumental Courante. Altho the time signature in the last is 3/2, it will be noticed that the very first measure is in 6/4 and the second in 3/2 time. All three, however, begin with an eighth note up-beat, as all Courantes should properly begin.

[41]

As the Galliard followed the Pavans, so the Couranta, in Germany, was the *Abtanz (Proporz)* after the *Haupt-Tanz (Allemands)*. It thus achieved the position of the second movement in the four-part classic Suite (formed about 1620); the basic pillars of which were the Allemande, Courante, Sarabande and Gigue. As such, (when the Suite evolved into the four-part Sonata) its form and characteristics became the germ for the Scherzo, or second movement of that important form. The Scherzo from Beethoven's *Fifth Symphony* (especially the Trio) is a good example in question.

The structural form of the Courante is made up of two parts, usually of 16 or 32 bars each. Modern composers have neglected the Courante; Walter Niemann and Cyril Scott being among the few who have written any. Bela Bartok (*Tre Correnti*) has transcribed three by Michelangelo Rossi (1630-1660), giving them a fuller and more modern texture.

Running plays an important role in the vocabulary of the modern dance, especially in group compositions, such as Martha Graham's *Course* and Doris Humphrey's *New Dance*. The Courante should prove a very useful medium for student investigation in such movement as leads to an interesting, formal and aesthetic employment of running motives in dance composition.

(*Lambranzi. New School of Theatrical Dancing.*)

SARABANDE

Sarabande

So you but with a touch of the hand
Turn all to Saraband.
(Lovelace, 1659.)

HOLDING the same position among 3/4 rhythms as the
Pavane does among the 4/4 variety, the Sarabande
likewise exhibits the same characteristics of gravity, pride,
solemnity, and (true to its Spanish ancestry) religious and
processional austerity. That it was adopted by the courts of
Europe at a later period than the Pavane is evidenced by the
fact that Arbeau (our great authority) does not mention it in
his *Orchesographie,* written in 1588. Despite this, however, it
seems to have been, in its original form, a much older dance,
being traced to the 12th century. It also seems to have
had a very dissolute youth, and we find many stories gathered
about its name. Its origin and derivation have given rise to
various surmises, but the majority of authorities claim for it
an Arabic-Moorish origin, explaining the etymology of its
name, in some instances, as from the Persian, *serbend*-song,
or again from the Persian, *sarband-a* fillet for a lady's head-
dress; also from the Moorish, *zarabanda*-noise. But we gain
the truest sense of its early life from a chapter "On the dancing and singing llamado Zarabanda" by Pedro Mariana
(1536-1623). He writes, "Amongst other inventions there has
appeared during late years a dance and song so lascivious in
its words, so ugly in its movements, that it is enough to inflame

[45]

even very modest people." He says it received its name at Seville from a fiend in a woman's form, and that its invention was one of the disgraces of the nation, causing more mischief than the plague. It became notorious as a dance of the courtesans, and during the reign of Philip II was for a time suppressed. It was, however, revived in a purer form, playing an important part in religious dramas. Fonta (*Introduction to French edition of Arbeau,* 1888) reproduces two hymns of the Mozarabian masses which were served by the chapters of the Cathedrals of Toledo and Seville, and the melody of a Sarabande by Boyer, (1630). Their characteristics are identical. As Fonta says, "the hymns are of a choric rhythm and always on a ternary measure, and they give the ear the impression of the languorous rhythm of the Sarabande. The *Seises* in Seville of our period are nothing but a continuation of the tradition of these masses and of the dances which accompanied the religious fetes."

It was introduced at the French court about 1588, and came into fashion when the melancholy Louis XIII (1601-1643) ascended the throne, and Spanish influence made itself known in France. The Chevalier de Grammont states that the music of this dance either delighted or annoyed people; the guitarists twanging it on their instruments till it was almost unbearable. "How they are tickl'd with a light ayre! The bawdy Saraband!" (Ben Jonson.)

However, at court it soon became a noble and solemn measure in spite of its being often danced with castanets. This is clearly shown in the accompanying print from Lambranzi's *New School of Theatrical Dancing,* (1716). History also relates of Cardinal Richelieu that, to gain the favor of Anne of

[46]

ADAGIO.

SARABANDE
from Lambranzi's *New School of Theatrical Dancing.*
(Harmonized by Louis Horst.)

Austria, he danced a Sarabande before her, with bells on his feet, and castanets in his hands.

Roger Dukas, the modern French composer, has written a symphonic poem, *Sarabande,* for chorus and orchestra, based on the story of the noble de Yveteaux, who, when dying at the age of 80, called for a Sarabande so that his soul might pass away more easily. This work was performed recently in New York by Toscanini and the Philharmonic orchestra.

In the Sarabandes that have come down to us, we are hard put to discover (according to our notions) any traces of their Arabic origin, yet among the memoirs of an old English beau we find the following illuminating passage: "I remember that when Hamet ben Hadji, the Morocco ambassador, was in England, my mother danced a Sarabande before him with a pair of castanets in each hand, and that his Excellency was so delighted with her performance that, as soon as she had done, he ran to her, took her in his arms, and kissed her, protesting that she had half persuaded him that he was in his own country." (*Badminton Book of Dancing.*) Hawkins (*History of Music,* 1776) also writes "within the memory of persons now living, a Saraband danced by a Moor was constantly part of the entertainment at a puppet-shew."

The form of its music structure is simple, a slow air in 3/4 time, beginning, like the Pavane, definitely on *one;* and divided into two parts, of which the first is generally eight measures, and the second twelve measures in length. It usually ends on the second beat of the last measure. The manner of playing this music is quaintly described in Mattheson's *The Perfect Conductor* (1739): "We arrive at the Sarabanda with its characteristics of singing, of playing and of dancing. The same has no other passion to express than ambition; yet

[48]

MARTHA GRAHAM
in Sarabande

therein are higher sorts to be discerned, so that the dance-sarabanda finds itself in a more selected, and yet thereby a much more pompous state than the others; because it permits of no running notes, since the *grandezza* abhors such, and its severity is maintained."

It was adopted as the third movement of the Suite—and quite naturally assumed the position of the slow movement when the Suite evolved into the Sonata form. Many of the andantes in the Sonatas of Haydn, Mozart and other classic composers are distinctly derived from the Sarabande form. One of the oldest Sarabandes we have is one in canon form by Louis Couperin (1630-1660). Fuertes, in his *Historia de la Musica Espanola,* quotes a Sarabande for guitar, but supplies no date. After Gluck (1714-1787) we find no composers of Sarabandes until Satie, in 1887, wrote a set of three; strange, mystical pieces, suggestive of intense, religious austerity. Since then there have been many beautiful re-creations of this important form by modern composers. Especially to be mentioned are those by Debussy, Honegger, Vidal, Tansman, Reutter, and, among Americans, Henry Brant, Beryl Rubinstein, Lehman Engel, and Henry Cowell.

Of the dance itself, we are informed by the *Dictionnaire de Trevoux,* 1721, that it was really hardly more than a very grave Minuet, slow and serious and processional. Playford (*The Dancing Master,* 1703) cites the steps of a Sarabande, in which there is much advancing and retiring; four steps forward, four backward; couples walking between lines formed by the other dancers; and other simple evolutions. But no mention is made of castanets.

Like the modern composers, the modern dancers have been much attracted to this form. Martha Graham's *Sarabande* (music by Lehman Engel) is one of her masterpieces, and her latest dance, the stirring *Immediate Tragedy,* employs Henry Cowell's beautiful Sarabande for musical accompaniment. At the 1937 session of the Bennington School of the Dance, Jose Limon produced two group dances, *Sarabande for the Dead* and *Sarabande for the Living,* to Henry Clark's music. Hanya Holm has done a Sarabande to music by Harvey Pollins, and Berta Ochsner used Couperin's Sarabande *La Lugubre* for her *Study for a Borgia.* All students of dance composition should likewise find this form a grateful vehicle for choreographic ideas of serious, and also of social import. The contemporary tragedy in Spain should supply much deeply felt subject matter. The Sarabandes of Martha Graham and Jose Limon are quite definitely concerned with this tragic scene.

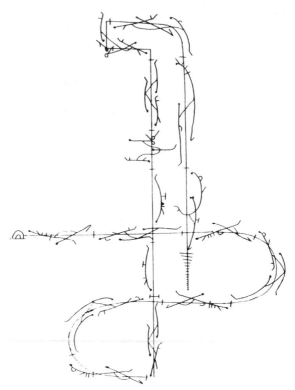

TRACT OF A SARABANDE
from *Feuillet*

IRISH JIG

(Wrightson)

Gigue

Sum luvis, new cum to toun,
With jeigis to mak thame joly;
Sum luvis to dance up and doun,
To meiss thair malancoly.
(Alexander Scott. *Ballat maid to
the Derision and Scorne of Wantoun Wemen.* 1560.)

"HOT and hasty like a Scotch Jigge" wrote Shakespeare, and, in one concise statement, the great bard disclosed the two outstanding characteristics of the Gigue. For it is certainly the quickest and most hasty of all the old dance forms; and if *hot* means exciting, it truly possesses the most exciting rhythmic urges of all music. This excitement is due, not only to its speed, but much more to its melodic basis, which we find to be in almost all cases, made up of rapidly moving groups of three notes. This produces the rhythm or pulse of the galop. Gigues are therefore mostly written in 3/8, 6/8, 9/8 or 12/8 time. Composers have often used this melodic and rhythmic formula when wishing to produce a quality of excitement; notably, Schubert in his famous song, *The Erl-King,* the pulse of which is exactly like that of a Gigue.

The Gigue is a very old dance, and probably belongs to many nationalities. Shakespeare might just as correctly have written "like an Italian, a Spanish, a French, or an English giga, gigue, or jig." But the earliest known ones have come to us from Italy, where it derived its name from *giga*—the name of a small stringed instrument. *Giga* also meant a leg, or limb. However the three greatest authorities on the Gigue, Werner Danckert, (*Geschichte der Gigue,* 1924), Jeffrey Pulver, (*The Origin of Jig,* 1917) and Charles Read Baskervill (*The Elizabethan Jig,* 1929), all claim an English origin for the dance, insisting that all earlier Italian uses of the word *giga* refer to the instrument only. Pulver traces this use of the word back as far as 1225, to the *Vocabulary* of John de Garlandia; "Giga est instrumentum musicum"; and also to the *Divine Comedy* of Dante (1265-1321):

> "Et come giga et arpa intempra tesa,
> Dimolte corde fa dolce tintinno."

These authorities claim that the use of the word in relation to dancing took place in England earlier than on the Continent. It also seems to have had its own etymology.

In Germany the common term for a violin is *Geige,* analogous to our term of *fiddle;* so it does not surprise us to find the fiddle the one instrument almost always associated with the Jigs of our own day. "As fidlers still, though they be paid to be gone, yet needs will thrust one more *iig* upon you." (Donne, 1593.)

It does not seem to have ever been a court dance, although all the famous court composers have written Gigues. Also Riche (1581) states that the Jig was established among the social dances of the nobility; and in 1591 we find one of the earliest examples of the sophisticated form of the music; Byrde's *A Galliards Gygge,* from *Lady Neville's Virginal Book.* English composers of the 16th century often called their Jigs a *Toy.* Also, these old English Jigs were not always in a three, six, nine or twelve-eighth rhythm. As often as not

GIGUE

J. P. Kirnberger. (1721-1783)

they were written, in just a lively 4/4 or 2/4 time. English literature of the 16th and 17th centuries fairly teems with references to the Jig, Ieig, Iyg, Iigge, Iygge, Iig, Ijyge, Gigge, Gig, Gygge, Jegg, etc. Playford, (in his *Dancing Master*, 1703) speaks of the sweet and airy activity of the gentlemen of the Inns of Court, who so greatly enjoyed the dancing of Jigs. But earlier, in 1674, this same Playford complains that "our late solemn musick is now jostled out of esteem by the new Corantos and Jigs of Foreigners." Nevertheless the Jig attained its greatest popularity in England, Scotland and Ireland; a popularity that has extended right down to our own time; especially in Ireland. Sir Henry Sidney, in a letter to Queen Elizabeth, in 1559, waxes enthusiastic over the dancing of Irish Jigs by the Anglo-Irish ladies of Galway, whom he describes as "very beautiful, magnificently dressed, and first-class dancers." (Flood. *History of Irish Music.* 1906.)

Kemp's Jigg as described by Playford, quaintly illustrates one of the most famous of the old English Jigs:

One man lead in two women forward and back:
Honour to one, honour to the other, then turn the third:
Lead your own with the left hand, and the woman you
    turned, and as much:
Then as much with the other second woman, turning your
    own:
The next man as much: Then the third as much:

First man lead the woman as before: turn half round holding
    both hands, and his own as much to the other, turn the
    third woman—
Do thus to all, the rest following and doing the like.
First man take the woman as before by the contrary hands
    behind, then lead them forwards and back, pull one half

[57]

AGNES DE MILLE
in Bach Gigue

about and kiss her, as much with the other, then the third. Do thus to all, the rest following and doing the like.

The accompanying engraving, by Wrightson, of an Irish Jig, not only shows us a goodly amount of excitement, but the necessary fiddler as well.

In the early English theatre it was customary to terminate a play with a Jig, accompanied by dancing and playing. "The Iyg at the end of an Enterlude, wherein some pretie knaverie is acted." In those days a Jig meant not only a dance, but a set of wanton verses as well. The word came to be synonymous with any light irreverent rhythm. In 1650 Thomas Mace wrote "Jiggs are light squibbish things only fit for fantastical light-headed people; and are of any sort of time." Halliwell says that the literary Jig was "a ludicrous metrical composition, often in rhyme, which was sung by the clown who occasionally danced, accompanied by the tabor and pipe."

In musical literature the Gigue holds an important place as the final movement of the Suite. From this position it evolved naturally into the closing movement of the Sonata form; many of the final movements of the Sonatas of Beethoven and other composers, being directly traceable to the Gigue, both in rhythm and tempo. The last movement of Beethoven's Violin Concerto is a notable example.

Mattheson draws his characteristic word-pictures in his endeavor to impart the texture of the music; "The common or English Gigues have as their distinguishing marks, an ardent and flying passion; a fury that quickly passes. The Italian Gigas, which are not made to be danced, but to be fiddled, drive themselves almost to the utmost speed or carelessness; yet, in the main, in a flowing and not violent manner; somewhat like a smooth shooting forth of the arrow-like torrent of a brook. To the ordinary gigue-tunes I can now apply four chief emotions; fury, or passion, pride, simple eagerness, and a careless temperament." (*Der Vollkommene Capellmeister*, 1739.)

In form the Gigue usually consisted of two sections, rather longer than those of the other dance forms, and was often written in a fugal style. Besides the great Gigues of Handel and Bach, there are splendid ones by Mattheson, Kirnberger, Lully, Loeillet, Graun, Zipoli and Rameau. There are a few by modern composers; Niemann has written one; but infinitely better is the *Giga* by Casella (from *Pieces Enfantines*) a raucous and ribald composition in the most ultra-modern idiom. The first of Debussy's three *Images* for orchestra is entitled *Gigues*. Richard Donovan's *Jig* from his *Suite for Piano* is a fine modern example by an American composer.

The Canary (supposedly from the Canary Islands) was a slower species of the Gigue; and the Loure (known sometimes as the Spanish Gigue) was a still slower variety. The frenetic Italian Tarantella possesses the same rhythmic and melodic structure as the Gigue, although much more peasant in character.

Among the contemporary dancers who have used this form, we must mention Agnes de Mille, whose excellent *Gigue* (to Bach's Gigue from the Fifth French Suite) is an outstanding work. It is quite obvious that this form should be suggested to all students for dance-studies of frenzy and tense excitement.

[60]

(*Tomlinson. Art of Dancing*)

MINUET

Minuet

Life is like a Minuet—
a few turns are made in order to curtsey
in the same spot from which we started.
(*Senac de Meilhan*)

ALTHOUGH to many of us the Minuet is probably
the least interesting of all the old dance forms (due to
its highly artificial and rococo character), nevertheless it attained the greatest popularity and degree of importance over
all the other dance forms. Mari Ruef Hofer says, "An attempt
to write all that the Minuet implies would necessitate com-
piling the social history of France during several centuries;
the manners, customs, costumes, art, music, and ceremonies
of the period of the Grand Manner, as well as the manifold
steps and forms invented in its behalf. Arriving as a climax
in the art of the dance, in a period of luxurious national life,
its very name suggests the refined magnificence of the courts
of the kings in whose century it flourished. Millions were spent
in its production; musicians, poets, decorators, artists and
costumers exercised their combined powers to set forth its
perfections. Its despotic ceremonial governed kings and
queens, and its etiquette decided the fate of statesmen more
often than their ability in statecraft. The dancing teachers of
that day were autocrats to whom all bowed and deferred."

Another reason for its importance lay in the fact that it was
the only dance form regularly admitted into the modern

Sonata form when this great form was evolved from the dance Suite; and this choice seems the more strange when we discover that the Minuet was not a charter member of the early Suite. We have seen that the basic members of the Suite were the Allemande, Courante, Sarabande and Gigue. A little later the composers began writing five- and six-part Suites, interpolating between the Sarabande and Gigue either one or two of the other forms. The Minuet was most often selected as the fifth member, but we find Gavottes, Bourrées, Rigaudons and Passepieds often introduced into the Suite. Because they were so inserted, these numbers were called *Intermezzi*. Mozart composed many symphonies in each of which appears a *menuetto*, with one exception; and this one is spoken of as the *Symphony without a Minuet*.

The great popularity of the Minuet is easily understood. It expressed more completely than any other dance the artificial behaviorism of the 18th century; and its short, mincing and dainty steps graphicly, and choreographicly, register for us the decline of the great French court, until it was engulfed by the French Revolution.

But the Minuet was not allowed to pass with the court. Just as Soviet Russia clings to the Ballet today so that new social order clung to the Minuet, and its existence was prolonged through most of the 19th century, until it was finally walked as a quadrille. This was especially the case among the pseudo-aristocracy of our Southern states. However, its terpsichorean sway was eventually usurped by the Waltz, and music fell heir to the duty of perpetuating the form.

Count Moroni states that in the Minuet is to be found the expression of that Olympian calm and universal languor which characterized everything of that period. Dancing was

OLDEST MINUET. (1653)
J.-B. Lully. (1633-1687)

not even called *dancing,* but was spoken of as *tracer les chiffres d'Amour* (tracing the figures of Love) ; and even *violin* was too commonplace a name. Musical instruments were called *les ames des pieds* (the souls of the feet).

Scott, in his work *The Art of Dancing,* writes that the rules concerning the Minuet would fill a volume, but that there were five requisites for making a good figure in this dance—a languishing eye, a smiling mouth, an imposing carriage, innocent hands and ambitious feet. Another famous dancing master said that he knew nothing of the Minuet although he had devoted his whole life to the study of it; on hearing which, Hogarth exclaimed he was glad he was a painter. Additional evidence of the popularity the Minuet attained in England is gathered from Macaulay's *History of England*: "Her authority was supreme in all matters of good breeding, from a duel to a Minuet," and from Lord Chesterfield who advised that one "should do everything in minuet time."

In Italy the Minuet was mainly treated with satire. In the drama and opera it was used to give comic relief; to typify all things that were ridiculously romantic or affectedly noble and stately. This use of the Minuet throws an interesting sidelight which helps to show how popular and widespread a form it had become.

Even in France everyone was desirous of affecting certain airs that would guarantee attracting general attention. These produced a so-called *Minuet position*—a kind of *dancing-step,* an apparent *melancholy,* a somewhat *dreaming-attitude,* a *short, tripping manner,* and a *parade-like swing* in conducting a lady to table. All these affected and even ridiculous points were then demanded as a matter of the greatest importance and necessity.

[65]

DORIS HUMPHREY and CHARLES WEIDMAN
in Minuet from Alcina Suite

The Minuet was originally a *Branle of Poitou;* it was quite gay, and contained fast movements. However, it underwent the usual changes after being introduced at the court of France in 1650, and became a dance of only moderate gayety and tempo. The Paris Dancing Academy became jealous of its sudden popularity which threatened to eclipse the fame of the Courante, greatly patronised by the Academy. In order to placate the academicians the Minuet was early called *the daughter of the Courante.* But for 150 years its universal title was *The Queen of Dances.* The name *Minuet* came from the French: *menu;* Latin: *minutus,*=*small, neat,* since it was danced with such small, dainty steps and exaggerated preciseness.

The musical form of the Minuet is that of the usual two-part dance form, cast in a moderate three-quarter time. We often find Minuets with a third part, or trio. Although it sometimes commences on the up-beat, in most cases it begins on the down beat;*i.e.* on *one.* As a member of the Sonata form, it was developed much more freely and its tempo was often increased, thereby producing a sort of Scherzo.

There were four very famous Minuets: *Le Menuet du Dauphin, Le Menuet de la Reine, Le Menuet d'Exaudet,* and *Le Menuet de la Cour.* The steps of these are fully described in Mari Ruef Hofer's *"Polite and Social Dances."* Some of the great ballet masters who played an important part in the creation of these various Minuets were Gardel, (who created the *Menuet de la Reine* for the nuptials of Louis XVI and Marie Antoinette,) Pécour, Exaudet, Rameau and Marcel. It was Marcel, the most famous of all the teachers of the Minuet who would often exclaim, "Que de choses dans un menuet!" (What a lot of things in a Minuet!)

[67]

Fine musical settings are too numerous to mention. Just as more has been written about the Minuet than any of the other old forms, so, likewise, more Minuets have been composed than any other musical form. There is no great composer since 1650, who has not written one or more. Excellent examples must actually run into the thousands. There is a very "embarrassment of riches." To Lully goes the honor of writing the first Minuet in 1653, a quaint little one in D minor. The modern composers (especially Satie, Ravel, Debussy, Casella, Prokofieff and Schoenberg) have also presented us with some fine settings.

Modern dancers have not followed in the foot-steps of the modern composers; but Doris Humphrey and Charles Weidman have given us an excellent choreographic presentation of Handel's *Alcina Suite,* in which they perform a very piquant and amusing Minuet.

The best use to be made of this form by the student in dance composition is for the development of a delicate satiric vein, produced through the smallest possible movements.

GAVOTTE

Gavotte

Arbeau: "You will find no great trouble in the *Branles de Gavottes,* in which the damsels need not be raised in the air, but only kissed."

Capriol: "That is something which I could do easily and willingly, and for that reason I wish to learn and know them."

(*Orchesographie,* 1588)

THE GAVOTTE was originally a peasants' dance, the favorite of the natives of Gap, a district in the Upper Alps in the ancient province of Dauphine, in south-eastern France. It receives its name from this district of Gap, the natives of which were called Gavots. It was one of the many dances that were derived from the old *branles* (brawls), especially the so-called *Branles Doubles,* and its character was brisk, sparkling and lively.

Arbeau informs Capriol that "a Gavotte is a collection of several *Branles Doubles* which musicians have chosen and arranged in a sequence. . . . To this sequence they have given this name of *Gavottes.* They are danced in duple (2/2) time with little jumps in the manner of the *Branle da Haut Barrois,* and consist of a *double* to the right and a *double* to the left like the *Branle Commun.* But the dancers divide the *doubles,* both to the right and to the left by passages taken at will from the *Gaillardes.* When the dancers have danced a little, one of them, with his damsel, goes a little way apart and makes

GAVOTTE

J. S. Bach. (1685-1750)

several passages in the middle of the dance in the sight of all the others; then he comes to kiss all the other damsels, and all the young men kiss his damsel, and they return to their proper order. Some accord the privilege of kissing to the leader of the dance alone, and to the damsel who is his companion. And at the end, the damsel having a chaplet or posy, presents it to one of the dancers, who has to pay the musicians."

The Gavotte was introduced at the French Court in the sixteenth century, when, to amuse the royal circles, dances were done in the costumes of the provinces whence they came. Originally a dance in which there was much kissing and capering, the Gavotte took a fresh direction in its new and majestic surroundings. It lost much of its ready roughness, and in due course of time came to be characterized by a formality and stateliness, and still later by a stiffness and artificiality, that would have greatly astonished the Gavots. The kisses were gradually replaced by bouquets, and the general quality of the dance approached that of the rococo Minuet. For a time attaining the title of *la danse classique* it later became known as the *gavotte tendre*.

As Mari Ruef Hofer so aptly states (in *Polite and Social Dances*), "the Gavotte appeared as a welcome reaction after a long period of strenuous etiquette devoted to dances of undoubtedly tedious elegance. One can fancy a younger generation of royalty seizing with avidity upon this new terpsichorean delight. It soon became the fashion to follow the stately measure of the old dance of ceremony, with the lighter and more vivacious graces of its rival. Who could divine that this pleasant breaking away from the stern formalities of court and caste might presage so dire and devastating a calamity as the not far distant French Revolution?"

[72]

MUSETTE

J. S. Bach. (1685-1750)

This devitalization of the dance to suit the more and more romantic ideas and tastes of each succeeding generation continued right down to our own day, until the Gavotte became synonymous with all that was overly sweet and sentimental. This fate of the Gavotte, and also of the Minuet, was due to their retention by the classic and romantic schools of music and dancing of the 19th century, whereas all the other forms were fortunately neglected and allowed to preserve inviolate for us most of their original distinction and beauty.

The form of the music is the usual two-part dance form, although in many cases we find a third part (or trio) the character of which is always rustic, and which is built upon a drone-bass in imitation of a bag-pipe. This part is called the Musette from *Cornemuse,* the French name for bag-pipe. We occasionally encounter a Musette among the Minuets and Bourrées but it does not occur in any of the other court forms. The Gavotte was often placed between the Sarabande and Gigue as the fifth or sixth member of the Suite.

It is written in a fast 2/2 or 4/4 time and has the outstanding rhythmic characteristic of beginning on the third quarter, which often results in a mild syncopation that is one of its charms. This matter of the two quarter note up-beats on 3 and 4, becomes increasingly important when we examine two other dance forms, the Bourrée and Rigaudon. They are both similar to the Gavotte, and are also conceived in a fast 2/2 or 4/4 time, but are each easily distinguishable by their opening up-beats. The Bourrée should properly begin with one quarter note up-beat on 4, the Rigaudon with an up-beat of two eighth notes on 4. Mattheson (*The Perfect Conductor,* 1739) has the following admonitions for the directors and composers of his time concerning the Gavotte: "Its emotion is truly a

[74]

real exultant joy. Its time-measure is indeed of an even sort but such a one as consists of two half beats; even though it, at the same time, allows itself to be divided into quarters; yes, even into eighths. I would wish that this distinction were taken heed of a little better, and that one would not be able to call most of them a *bad measure;* as does happen. The hopping character is a legitimate property of these Gavottes; by no means the running. I seem to see these mountain folk jumping about on the hills with their Gavottes."

But another peasant folk (on the extreme north-west coast of France) took to the Gavotte with great zeal. This was in the province of Brittany, where the dance was known as the *Gavotte Bretonne.* Charbonnel (in *La Danse*) relates that it flourished with the greatest enthusiasm during the season of marriages which in this region are all held at the same time. Then one can see in the squares and along the streets, interminable processions of dancers giving themselves up to their favorite dance with gusto. It even seems that they go at it with such ardor that the department of streets and bridges is obliged to repave the streets cut up by the vigorous feet of the Breton dancers.

Of the court dance itself, there are many instructions left us by famous ballet masters, notably those of Gardel, de Vestris and Littre. Gardel created the famous *Gavotte le Ballet du Roi.* Littre says: "The Gavotte step differs only from the natural walking step in that one springs upon the foot which is on the ground, and at the same time points the toe of the foot downward." De Vestris describes it as consisting chiefly of "three steps and an assemblé."

The oldest Gavotte may be found in the *Orchesographie,* (1588) but both the music and the figures are unsuitable to

[75]

the later forms and customs, as they deal with a period prior to the introduction of the Gavotte at court. Arbeau records the inadequacy of his own material when he says, "If this type of dance had been in fashion when my legs were young I should not have failed to make notes about it."

Among the finest Gavottes by the old masters are those by Bach, Telemann, Kirnberger, Foerster, Graupner, Rameau and Handel. Our great modernist, Prokofieff, has composed three highly interesting models, one in the boisterous rustic manner (op. 32 no. 3), another in the classic style (from *Symphonie Classique,* op. 25) and one in the later hot-house or salon genre (op. 12 no. 2). Karganoff, Lopatnikoff and Schoenberg have also produced compositions in this form. Martha Graham used the Schoenberg *Gavotte and Musette* a few seasons ago for a dance entitled *Phantasy.*

LA BOURRÉE

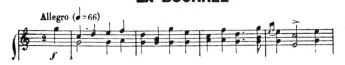

Bourrée

From hence came all those monstrous stories
That to his lays wild beasts danc'd borees.
(Jonathan Swift, *Ovidiana*.)

THOUGH possessed of an entirely original and independent character, the Bourrée, nevertheless, forms one of a family of three old dances, whose general musical design was mentioned in the analysis of the Gavotte. Three dances, (the Gavotte, the Bourrée, and the Rigaudon) are all in a lively 2/2 or 4/4 time, but each one has its own distinctive manner of beginning, that has much to do with establishing its particular character.

The Gavotte, originally of quite a hearty and vigorous calibre, begins with two up-beats on the third and fourth quarters; thereby losing a little of its strength through the delayed entrance of its primary accent. The Bourrée properly begins with one up-beat on the fourth quarter. This more sudden approach to its primary accent contributes, no doubt, to its having greater vigor and lustiness than the Gavotte possesses. The Rigaudon also begins on the fourth quarter, but this quarter should be broken into two eighth notes up-beats. This presupposes a more general use of eighth notes throughout the entire form, which would have much to do with producing the generally light and superficial character that the Rigaudon possesses.

To say that the Bourrée is hearty and full of energy is not

[78]

enough. It is the most vigorous and earthy among the old dance forms. The origin of the word itself is uncertain. According to one authority, Bourrée is defined as a bundle of small pieces of wood. This etymology is corroborated by Lapaire (in his *La Bourrée, Paris,* 1921): "The Bourrée dates, it would seem, from historic Gaul. It arose perhaps from some Gallic festival, the *Jour des Fagots,* for example, when our ancestors danced with flaming torches on the heights, around huge fires."

Mattheson (*Der Vollkommene Capellmeister,* 1739) gives us his customary qualified facts: "The word Bourrée in itself really means something stuffed, filled out, sedate, strong, weighty, and yet soft or delicate;—which is more adapted to shoving, sliding, and gliding than to hopping and jumping. This is in agreement with the qualities of the Bourrée, namely: content, pleasant, untroubled, tranquil, listless, gentle,— and yet agreeable. Since there is now a well-known dance which in honor of a bride is called *la mariee,* it might well be that the people of Biscay, where the Bourrée is quite at home, and where there are seldom any plump pretty figures, imported this dance to please somewhat that sort of woman and named it that. Truly it lends itself to no type of figure better than to an undignified one. However, these are only conjectures which for the most part tend to perplexity."

It was originally a peasants' dance; a rustic clog-dance of the natives of Auvergne and Berri, provinces in the mountainous region of central France. Marius Versepuy, an Auvergnat musician, who has given us many collections of Bourrées, writes: "The Bourrée constitutes a veritable little scenario of which love is the theme. It would be difficult to give an idea of the Bourrée except to say that the dancers seek and flee

[79]

(*Charbonnel. La Danse.*)

LA BOURREE AUVERGNAT

from each other. However, the roles are different. The man, bold and proud, dances with a determined air, stamping and clapping and shouting. The woman, at once audacious and timid, attracts her admirer and avoids him, using calculated ruses and tender artifices. One appears earnest, the other coquettish. The couples mix, cross, swinging the head and body, raising the arm, snapping their fingers, and noisily hammering out with their feet the beat given out by the bag-pipes or the hurdy-gurdy. Rhythm is essential in the Bourrée —to the point where it alone suffices. In the absence of the bag-pipe, one may see one of the dancers perched on a table singing the air while he vigorously pounds out the rhythm with his foot. Finally his humming diminishes, he no longer sings. His heel suffices to keep the couples going until dawn."

Longy, another authority, describes a more formal variety of the peasant Bourrée: "The men—an indeterminate number —place themselves in a line, the women in another, each man opposite his partner. They move together, forward and back, a certain number of times; the first man at the right then goes across to the women's side and the lady on the opposite end joins the line of men; then they again go forward and back, the first man on the right and the last lady on the left make the same figure as the ones before. It continues thus until each has had his turn; then the dance is finished and each man kisses his partner. The dancers shout, beat with their hands and feet, particularly when they cross over to change sides."

It was also sung and danced to the rhythmic labor of the wine-makers when crushing the grapes by stamping (or dancing) upon them with their bare feet. A Parisian writer of the past century reports "how the clumsy Auvergnat, the tradi-

ALLEGRO

BOURREE. (from *Phaeton*)

J.-B. Lully. (1633-1687)

tional Paris water-carrier and porter, becomes lively and bright when he dances the Bourrée; how his heavy frame moves in cadence, and how the clogs fall together with precision, while an occasional shout of 'yow-yow' is heard." A typical verse from one of the many sung Bourrées follows:

> When you marry
> Know what you are taking;
> If you take her young
> The coocoo will sing;
> If you take her old,
> He will already have sung.

The Bourrée was introduced at the Court of France, in 1565, during the reign of Catherine de Medici. There it was danced with many crossing steps (*tres croise*) and cuts (*coupe*). The dancers stood opposite one another and executed various steps, such as *pas de bourrée ouvert, pas de bourrée emboité,* and *pas de fleurets.* These were all crossing steps. The *coupé* (or cut) was usually performed on the quarter note up-beat. As Lapaire says, "It made Marquis and Marquise lift a foot." It is also stated that it was a dance of careless form, done with much skipping. This coincides with the description of the Bourrée (as a music form) by the German musicologist, Schubert, who states that "the character of its melody has something of calmness, freedom from worry and amiable carelessness in its essence." Gaston Vuillier writes that the third beat of each measure was accentuated with exaggerated vehemence by the stamping of the feet. Although mentioned by Sevigné and Chateaubriand, the Bourrée never became a popular dance at court. It is not difficult to understand this lack of enthusiasm, especially when we remember the rough rusticity of the measure. De Felice (in 1770) says "it was little employed because its steps were not noble enough for the theatre or opera." However, Lully, Destouches, Marais and Rameau all included Bourrées in many of their operas and ballets. One of the most used steps in the ballet, is still known as the *pas de Bourrée*.

That it was early danced in England can be learned from Playford's *Musick's Delight* (1666), which contains three pieces labeled *Bore, Boree* and *A Running Boore*. In his *Dancing Master* (1703) he also gives the steps of an *Irish Boree*.

It soon disappeared from the dancers' repertoire, and we later find it only in the Suite where the guest's place (between the Sarabande and Gigue) was often open to receive it. The composers frequently followed the first Bourrée with a second one; and sometimes this second Bourrée is *a la Musette*.

There have been many fine Bourrées written by the old masters; especially by Bach, Fasch, Stölzel, Handel and Kuhnau. The greatest of them all is the famous Bourrée from the *Second Violin Sonata* of Bach.

Despite its direct and vigorous appeal, not many modern composers of note have been inspired by this form. The only modern Bourrées (and those only comparatively modern) known to the writer, are by Lachaume, Chabrier and Edward German. The one by Lachaume is the last movement of a suite called *Trianon,* and, strangely enough, this movement is designated as a Gavotte-Bourrée. But in reality it is a Bourrée, beginning with a good, healthy up-beat on the fourth quarter. The one by Chabrier is called *Bourrée Fantasque,* and the Bourrée by German was written for a production of Shakespeare's *Much Ado About Nothing.*

Arthur Mahoney is perhaps the only contemporary dancer employing this form. A *Bourrée,* in the elaborate style of the *Ballet de Cour,* is one of his most effective dances.

[84]

ARTHUR MAHONEY
in Bourrée

RIGAUDON

Rigaudon

Let us go to Bordeaux
My little Jeannette,
Let us go to Bordeaux
While the weather is nice.
There we shall eat an omelette,
And there we shall dance a rigaudon.
    (*Old Provence Song*)

J OHANN MATTHESON, (in his *Der Vollkommene Capellmeister,* 1739) supplies the most interesting, and also the most debatable information concerning the Rigaudon. He writes: "This melody, to my judgment, is one of the most agreeable. Its individuality springs from a somewhat frivolous pleasantry. The Rigaudon was often used by the Italians as a closing chorus in dramatic works; by the French for the singing of particular odes and pleasing ariettas. Regarding its form, it must be noted that the third part must almost represent an insertion or Parenthesis, as if it did not belong at all to the composition, but rather as if it had almost entered by chance: therefore this third and shorter movement, must also be lower in tonality and must have no definite ending, so that the return to the beginning strikes the ear so much the fresher.

"For the rest the Rigaudon is actually a hybrid, constructed from the Gavotte and Bourrée, and could rightly be called a four-part Bourrée. However, the details and the form, the

[87]

divisions, the compass, the changes are constructed quite differently.

"In the olden days this dance was called, in Italian, *Rigo,* which means a river or stream, and I find it true that it is traditional with seafaring people. There is a well-known Sailor's-Rigaudon that commences with the words *Dans nos Vaisseaux etc.* Richelet says the Rigaudon came from Provence, and I believe it the more readily, because the Mediterranean Sea provides the intercourse with Italy."

Mattheson is right about the "frivolous pleasantry" of the Rigaudon, as it is assuredly the lightest and most shallow of all the old dance forms. We have seen that the Gavotte has two quarter note up-beats on 3 and 4, and that the Bourrée begins with a quarter note up-beat on 4. The Rigaudon (likewise in a lively 2/2 or 4/4 time) also begins on the fourth quarter but this quarter note should properly (although there are many exceptions) be divided into two eighth notes. A composition beginning thusly with two eighth notes will naturally contain a large proportion of notes of similar value in the main body of the work; and this predominance of shorter notes has much to do with creating the character of lightness and brittleness inherent in the Rigaudon.

Matheson may again be correct in believing that the Rigaudon came from Italy *via* Provence, but most authorities feel it to be truly French, and claim it was originally a gay peasant dance of Provence and Languedoc, sung and danced to the rhythmic accompaniment of the tambourine. Also, these authorities hold that it owes its name to a famous ballet master of Marseilles, named Rigaud who brought it to Paris, during the reign of Louis XIII (1601-1643), where it met with great favor.

The light and brilliant qualities of the Rigaudon appealed in particular to the skillful dancers at the French court and tempted them towards the interpolation of many virtuoso steps during the course of the dance. From this to its general use as the vehicle for most of the brilliant solos of the operas and ballets of the period was only a logical step. Long after its popularity had waned as a court dance, it still was regarded as the ideal accompaniment for exhibition dancing. This was also quite logical, for the predominant little groups of eighth notes were most suitable for the many brilliant, light and flickery steps that made up most of the virtuoso ballet dancer's vocabulary.

Of the dance itself, Campan and Isaac give us directions that include much running, hopping and turning; also *balancés* made with quick little steps. As Desrat says in his *Dictionnaire de la Danse,* "the light music bears witness to the similar character of the dance."

It also had a great vogue in England, where the name was anglicized to Rigadoon. In Playford's *Dancing Master,* (1703) there is the description of a very short dance he calls: *The Last New French Rigadoon*:

> "The first man cast off and go half round—the second couple do the same—then back to back with your partners and turn—then back to backsides, and turn sides and cast off."

Its popularity there supports Mattheson's statement that it was really a sailor's dance. For, when we examine any English Hornpipe, we find it is invariably built like a Rigaudon. The *St. Catherine Rigadoon* by John Barrett (1674-1735) is a true Hornpipe; and a modern English composer, Dalhousie Young, has written a *Rigaudon for Piano,* sub-titled *Sailor's*

[89]

Hornpipe. That Oscar Wilde was cognizant of the extremely light character of this dance was shown when he selected it for dramatic contrast to sombre death in his *Ballad of Reading Gaol,* where he limns the picture of a hanged criminal dancing a Rigadoon of death with his heels upon the empty air.

The music is in the usual two-part dance form, but there are many examples of Rigaudons written in pairs, the second one practically serving as a trio. When joined in this fashion, we find that if one, for instance, is in E major, the other will be in E minor. But we do not discover in these trios any of the strange things that Mattheson would lead us to expect. He also states that the Rigaudon is a hybrid, and then, contradicting himself, finds its characteristics quite different from either the Gavotte or Bourrée. The Rigaudon has its own true type, and while it may be true that it resembles the Bourrée, it can be just as fairly said that the Bourrée resembles the Rigaudon. Composers did not observe enough the distinction between these two forms. Even such a master as Bach wrote his Bourrées as often with two eighth note up-beats as he did with a quarter note up-beat. And other composers have given us many Rigaudons beginning (*a la Bourrée*) with a quarter note up-beat. But the finest Rigaudons, such as the two by Rameau, commence properly. The Rigaudon is only occasionally found in the Suite.

Among modern composers who have written in this form are Prokofieff, Percy Pitt, Dellanoy, Saint-Saëns and Niemann. Strangely enough, our American romanticist, Edward Mac Dowell, has written one which is quite free in form and full of New England woodsy and whimsy but nevertheless a Rigaudon.

[90]

ALLEGRO.

RIGAUDON
J. P. Kirnberger. (1721-1783)

Among modern dance compositions the only use made of the Rigaudon form that comes to mind is an extremely humorous and satiric group dance, *Exhibition Piece;* the choreography by Marian Van Tuyl, the music a Rigaudon by Jean Williams.

(*Ardern Holt*)

PASSEPIED

Passepied

The passe-pied of Callac,
The passe-pied simple.
Whoever will do this
Must be a man.
(Couplet de Passe-pied.)

NEXT to the Rigaudon, the Passepied is probably the lightest of the old court forms. But, whereas the former reflects a decided shallowness, the Passepied possesses a lightness of deeper import approaching the more solid gayety inherent in the Galliard. There is no more apt description of it than that given by Johann Mattheson, the great German musicologist and composer, in his *Der Vollkommene Capellmeister* (1739). His instructions to the conductors of his day as to the proper method of conducting this form are as follows: "There still belongs to the lively melodies *Le Passepied*. Its character comes quite near to frivolousness, for the ardour, the anger or the passion that one encounters in a flying Gigue is surely not to be found in the restlessness and fickleness of such a Passepied. However, it is yet such a kind of frivolousness as contains nothing odious or displeasing, rather much more something agreeable; just like some women, who, even though somewhat inconstant, do not, however, lose their charm thereby."

In the old days every French province had its *Branle,* and the Passepied was the *Branle of Brittany,* where it was also called Trihoris. It is under the name of Trihory that we find a short description of it in Arbeau's *Orchesographie* (1588), but no mention of the word "passepied." It was an ancient pantomimic dance, and real dramatic talent was required for its performance.

Fonta says that "it was really a gay and charming dance; the sameness of the movement of always keeping the right foot in front and sliding and stretching it out along the ground, in the manner of the paws of a young cat, rendered the dance coquettishly pleasant." (*Introduction to French edition of Arbeau,* 1888.) The feet crossed and recrossed each other in the many gliding steps: hence its name. Trevoux's *Dictionnaire* (1721) describes the movement of the feet with the words, *pedum decussatus.* Praetorius (*Terpsichore,* 1612) says "the Passepied is so named because in such a dance one must beat and place one foot over the other." Despereaux states, "the light Passepied ought to fly close to the ground." One of the common expressions was to "run a Passepied."

The dance itself usually consisted of ten figures. It started with the dancers facing each other with joined hands, then setting to each other with a *Pas de Basque,* bringing the left shoulder forward, then the right, and changing places with a turning step. Another figure consists of the dancers making pirouettes with eight pony steps pawing the ground; also this was supposed to be done with their arms around each others necks.

Originally danced by the Breton peasants it found great favor in court circles during the reign of Louis XV, when pastoral entertainments, (*paysanneries*) were given at every opportunity. At these festivities the lords and ladies disguised themselves as shepherds and shepherdesses. Madame de

[95]

Sevigné was known for her excellence in the Passepied. In a letter to her daughter (in 1671) she writes "I am sure that you would be enraptured to see Lomaria dance the Passepied, and the violins of the court would make your heart ache. I wish you could see the manner in which M. de Lomaria lifts and replaces his hat. What grace! What precision! The Passepied could make me weep because it brought back to me such sweet memories which it was impossible for me to resist." M. de Lomaria became famous for his dancing of the Passepied, and the grace displayed by him in the course of raising and replacing his hat caused the Passepied to become a dance with a hat. There is also a letter from the French king, Henry IV, to M. du Plessio-Mornay, November 1597, to which he adds the postscript: "I shall be at Blois the 16th of next month without fail, fully resolved to learn the Passe-pied of Brittany. Henry."

In England this dance was known as the Paspe, also as the Papsy. Playford (in *Dancing Master,* 1703) gives us the following plan for a Paspe—

"First couple cross over to the second *improper,* then the figure through the second couple to the second *proper,* then cross over to the third *improper,* then the first couple cast up to the second *improper,* and cross over below the second couple to the first *improper,* then the first and second women change places, and the first and second man the like, then the first and second couple all hands half around, and the first couple cast off to the second *improper,* then the first woman cross over below the third woman and come between the third couple (the first man at the same time cross over and go above second man and so between the second couple) then the first woman in the middle of the third couple hands

[96]

VIVACE.

PASSEPIED
(from *L'Europe Galante*.) André Campra. (1660-1744)

all three abreast (the first man the same with the second couple at the same time), then meet and set, then the first man hand his own and turn to the second *proper.*"

(*Proper* is when the men and women are on their own sides. *Improper* is when the men are on the women's side, or the women on the men's side.)

There is also a rare work entitled *The Passepied Round O,* (rondo?) *A New Dance Compos'd and written into Characters in the year 1715* by Kellom Tomlinson, dancing master.

The musical form of the Passepied consists of two or four parts of 8 or 16 measures in a fairly rapid 3/8 time, beginning with an eighth note up-beat. If in four parts, the first two parts are mostly in major, and the last two in minor. In many of them we find a characteristic use of syncopation (usually in the cadences) where three definite rhythmic accents are brought forth in two measures of three counts each, on 1, 3 and 2. (*i.e.* 1 2 3, 1 2 3.) As the tempo is quite lively this syncopation proves an effective rhythmic device.

Authorities often mention the Passepied in contrast to the Minuet. In reality, it is musically more like a Waltz, seeming to be its parent. Many of the Passepieds by German composers, especially those by Telemann, Foerster and Starzer, sound very much like a German Ländler. Occasionally we find Passepieds in the classic Suites; fine ones by Bach appear in his *Fifth English Suite* and in his *Fifth Partita.* Other interesting examples are those by Campra, Destouches, Kirnberger, Grünewald, Handel, Couperin and Rameau. Three Passepieds by modern composers (Debussy, Delibes and Lachaume) possess all the characteristic lightness of this dance, but, are written in 2/4 time. This is a return to the ancient

[98]

meter, as many of the original peasant Passepieds (such as the *Trihory de Bretagne* in Arbeau's *Orchesographie*), were in a binary rhythm. A Passepied by Percy Turnbull, 1925, is in the classic 3/8 time.

TRACT OF A CHACONNE

from *Feuillet*.

Chaconne and Passacaglia

THE reason for examining these two forms simultaneously does not arise from any belief that they were not different dances. Actually they were different, but musically, they developed along identical lines into four distinct and large forms, three of which are among the most important in musical composition. Musicologists are today still at variance when attempting to distinguish the two forms, but we do know that in the court days the Chaconne was the more important of the two and its dance form was largely responsible for the resultant musical forms; whereas today the most significant of these four musical forms is known as the Passacaglia form.

The Chaconne was undoubtedly of early Spanish origin; a slow solemn dance in 3/4 time; a theatrical dance much like a Sarabande. The accompanying print from Lambranzi's *New School of Theatrical Dancing* (1716) gives us a Chaconne with the following scenario beneath it: "A Gypsy is dancing a Cicona alone, with castanets in her hands. . . . A necromancer enters and touches her with his wand. She becomes transfixed while he dances alone; finally they both dance together to the end." Also, in *Don Quixote*, Cervantes writes that it was a mulatto dance done by negroes and negresses imported by the French for that purpose.

It is difficult to admit the etymology of the name as the definitions offered by the ancient authorities are so widely at variance as to cause the student more confusion than enlightenment. Mattheson (*Der Vollkommene Capellmeister,* 1739) only adds more confusion: "The largest among these dance forms is indeed the Ciacona, or Chaconne, with its brother, or its sister, the Passagaglio, or Passacaille. I find that Chaconne is really a family name, and that the admiral of the Spanish fleet in America, *anno* 1721, was named Mr. Chacon. Such a derivation satisfies me more than that one, in a certain dictionary, which derives from Persian chess. The Chaconne is sung and danced, sometimes at the same time; and even if such diversions are alternated, there yet is expressed considerable pleasure; however at all times more satiation than savour. One knows how easily satiation brings forth disgust and aversion; and whoever would wish to produce these emotion-movements, need only order a pair of Chaconnes thereto; so would the matter be correct." This interpretation is decidedly different from the majestic and solemn emotion usually evoked upon hearing a Chaconne by one of the masters of that period.

It was adopted by the French and transformed by them into a social dance. It became the concluding dance of a ball; the dancers forming two lines, the gentlemen on one side, the ladies on the other. First they all danced for eight bars then a couple (or small group) performed different figures, usually down and back between the two lines. Then the entire assembly would again dance the first figure, after which a second couple (or group) would perform another different figure, followed again by the opening figure. The dance continued in this alternate fashion until each couple had performed its individual figures, and finally all the dancers met together for a last repetition of the opening figure. Important musical developments arose from these rather simple evolutions.

[102]

(*Lambranzi. New School of Theatrical Dancing.*)

CHACONNE

Of necessity the first to arise was simply a more extended composition. Instead of the usual two-part dance form (with occasionally a third part, or trio) the early Chaconnes consisted of 4, 5, 6 or more parts, often covering 4 or 5 printed pages. Among Chaconnes of this relatively unimportant type are those by Lully and Blow. Passacaglias of this class have been written by Lalande, Gervais and Roncalli, the latter transcribed into a modern setting by Respighi.

Another inevitable outgrowth was a rich exposition of the rondo form (*A-B-A-C-A-D-A-E-A, etc.*) On the recurrences of the *A* section the entire group danced, while the couples performed their various individual figures on the *B-C-D-E, etc.* In fact, the Chaconnes of this genre have these sections designated as *1st couplet, 2nd couplet;* one by François Couperin contains eight couplets. Louis Couperin and d'Anglebert have also written Chaconnes in this rondo form. Besides the above mentioned Chaconnes there is also a fine *Passacaille en rondeau* by Francois Couperin.

A third development was the "theme and variation" type of Chaconne or Passacaglia. This undoubtedly came from the musicians themselves. Playing the same eight bars over and over again, it was inevitable that they would gradually begin to variate the melody, if only to relieve the tedium of monotony. Among the examples of this class we have a Chaconne by Pachelbel with 13 variations, and two by Handel (one with 21, the other with 62 variations). Though not so entitled Beethoven's "32 variations on a theme in C Minor" is a pure Chaconne. Handel's famous Passacaglia also belongs in this category.

The fourth and most important form developed logically from the third as a series of variations on a ground bass; *i.e.,* an ever-recurring phrase in the bass, usually eight bars in length. Such a bass is also called *Basso Ostinato* (obstinate bass). Among musicians this is now known as the Passacaglia form, and it has become one of the grandest devices of their creative craft.

In this group we find the finest works of the masters; notably the Chaconnes of Pachelbel, Purcell, Couperin, Frescobaldi and Bach. Also Passacaglias by the same composers. The modern examples (all Passacaglias) include those of Scott, Bax (*Paean*), Hindemith (from *Der Demon*), Percy Grainger (*Green Bushes*), Blanchet (*Tocsin*) and Aaron Copland.

The confusion regarding these two forms among early musicologists has been admirably described by the annotator in the program of a recent concert by the Philadelphia Symphony Orchestra. He writes as follows:

"Schweitzer remarks that "it is very instructive to compare Bach's Chaconne with his Passacaglia, which is also in reality a Chaconne"; and he proceeds to distinguish as follows the two forms: "The Chaconne and Passacaglia are derived from old dance forms, and are characterized by the fact that they are developed out of an ever-recurring theme of eight bars in ¾ time. In the Chaconne, this theme may appear in all the parts; in the Passacaglia, it is confined to the bass.

"But now listen to the learned author of the article 'Passacaglia' in *Grove's Dictionary*: 'The only material difference between the two forms appears to be that in the Chaconne the theme is kept invariably in the bass, while in the Passacaglia it is used in any part'—a distinction, it will be observed, precisely the opposite of that made by Schweitzer.

"Certain of the older theorists, on the other hand, assert that the two terms are virtually interchangeable. De Bros-

MODERATO.

CHACONNE. (With 62 Variations)
G. F. Handel. (1685-1759)

MODERATO

PASSACAILLE. (Rondo)

Francois Couperin. (1668-1733)

sard, in his *Dictionnaire de Musique* (1703-1705) declares that 'the Passacaglia is properly a Chaconne. The only difference is that the pace is generally slower than that of the Chaconne.' J. G. Walther, in his *Musikalisches Lexikon* (1732) insists that 'the Passacaglia is inherently a Chaconne.' Mattheson (*Kern Melodischer Wissenschaft*, 1737) says that the two forms are 'brother and sister.'

"The puzzled student may therefore be excused for wondering whether Bach's Passacaglia is really a Chaconne (as it would seem to be, if we accept the definition of Schweitzer and others), and his Chaconne really a Passacaglia (as it is if we accept the definition of *Grove's Dictionary*); or whether both are Chaconnes, or both Passacaglias; or whether it is scarcely worth while to attempt to find out."

Of the Chaconne we learn that when the court tired of it, it found a place on the stage. It appears in the operas of Gluck as an extended finale. Desrat states that it was often done by women; the accompanying illustration shows a tract (by Feuillet, 1703) of a Chaconne for a woman. Desrat also states that the Passacaglia was a dance of imposing majesty often executed by a gentleman alone. Despereaux describes Louis XIV to us:

"In the costume of a God, dancing solo at Versailles,
With grave, majestic steps, the solemn Passacaille."

The etymology of Passacaglia is best defined by Larrousse as coming from the Spanish-*passacalle* (*Passar*—to pass, and *calle*—street)—"an air on the guitar which serenaders played in the streets as a means of seduction." Another interesting derivation is that given by Schubert who states that the name comes from *Passagallo,* meaning *cock-tread* or *cock-trot.*

Some Lesser Forms

CANARIES

ALTHOUGH often mentioned as a slower form of the Gigue, the Canaries must have been quite a lively dance in Shakespeare's day. In *Love's Labour Lost* (1588) we find:

"To Jigge off a tune at the tongues end, Canarie it with the feet." and in *"All's Well that Ends Well"* (1601):

"A medicine that's able to breathe life into a stone and make you dance Canari."

Mattheson (1739) writes that the Canaries display great eagerness and agility. Mabel Dolmetsch says the peculiarities of the Canaries are the heel and toe step, the stamp and the swishing slide.

It was probably derived from a mascarade or ballet representation of savages from the Canary Islands. It is in 3/8 or 6/8 time. The first crotchet (eighth note) of each triolet is dotted; giving the rhythm much more of a light lilt than the driving Gigue.

It is not found in the Suite, but often in the ballets of Lully, Campra, Destouches and Rameau. Francois Couperin, Chambonnieres and Purcell have also written Canaries.

[109]

LOURE

The Loure, known as the Spanish Gigue, is a slower species of Gigue, but does not replace, but precedes it, when used in the Suite. It is written in a rather slow 6/4 time. Mattheson says it is "proud and arrogant in manner, therefore it was much liked by the Spaniards." Scott (in *Dancing in all Times*) speaks of a solemn Louvre. Telemann and Kirnberger have written Loures; Rameau has a Loure in *Castor et Pollux* and another in *Platee;* and Bach precedes the Gigue in his *Fifth French Suite* with a Loure.

PASSAMEZZO

Grove's *Dictionary* states that the Passamezzo was, "an old Italian dance which was probably a variety of the Pavane. In England, where it was popular in Queen Elizabeth's time, it was sometimes known as *Passing Measures Pavan*. In a ms. volume of airs and dances by Strogus, Dowland and Reade, in the Cambridge University Library it is called *Passmezures Pavan*. Hawkins says that the name is derived from *passer,* to walk, and *mezzo,* middle or half, and that the dance was a diminutive of the Galliard; but both these statements are probably incorrect. Practonius says that a Galliard has five steps, and is therefore called a *cinquepas,* so a Passamezzo has scarcely half as many steps as the latter, and is therefore called the *mezzo passo.* These derivations seem somewhat far-fetched, and it is probable that the name *passe-mezzo* (in which form it is found in the earliest authorities) is simply an abbreviation of *Passo e mezzo; i.e.* step and half, which may have formed a distinctive feature of the old dance. Full directions for dancing the passamezzo may be found in Carosa da Sermoneta's curious works *Il Ballarino* (Venice 1581) and *Nobiltà di dame* (1600).

In the Fitzwilliam Virginal Book there is a Passamezzo Pavana by William Byrde and another by Phillips; both are written in an elaborate style, and followed by a Galiarda-Passamezzo.

Arbeau tells us that "the musicians sometimes play it (the pavane) less gravely, and in this manner it partakes of the moderate tempo of a Basse-dance, when it is called passa-mezzo." But the most authentic explanation seems to be the following one by Mabel Dolmetsch: "Passo e mezzo is ar-ranged in the same plan as the Italian Pavans, but with half the proportion of steps in proportion to the bars of music, so that a step which would take one bar in the Pavan takes 2 in the passo e mezzo, and the music is played faster."

In Shakespeare's *Twelfth Night* we have the expression *a passy-measure pavyn.*

It had an easy quiet character and was much favoured by the Venetians.

ADDENDA ONE

Authentic Forms

THE PAVANE OF HENRY III

from Desrat's *Dictionnaire de la Danse*

The Pavane is danced to a slow measure in two beats, with the following step, made to the front, back, side, and turning.

STEP—

1st beat (the step described on the right foot). Bend both knees, sliding the right foot.

2nd beat—extend the left leg in front of the right, toe very pointed and the toe alone touching the floor.

(On the left foot, the step is the opposite. To turn, rise to the toe of the right foot, bringing the left foot close in front.)

FIGURES—

1st refrain—2 couples facing, gentleman at left of lady. Large semi-circle to their right to change places: pavane step to right.

Gentlemen hold their ladies' hands very high. After changing places, couples bow.

2nd refrain—The two couples do 4 pavane steps advancing to their right, stopping facing each other in the middle of the room. Bow. Advance towards each other by 2 pavane steps and pirouette on toe, each gentleman doing this with opposite lady. Gentleman turns back to face his own partner, and with 4 pavane steps they return to their places. In returning, the gentleman leads the lady with her right hand in his left. One beat taken on the toes, then a slow bow.

3rd refrain—One gentleman alone makes a large semi-circle to the left with 4 pavane steps. Arriving in front of the opposite lady, he performs a bow and curtsey with her. Returns to place over the same semi-circle. Bow and courtsey with his own lady. Second gentleman does the same.

Coda—The two couples advance without holding hands by 4 pavane steps opening to the right and the left; bow; gentleman turns to face partner, bows, returns her to place from which he invited her.

Pavane often ended in a promenade with bows as at beginning.

GALLIARD

from Arbeau's *Orchesographie*

A.
1. Grue gauche. (Coupé or Cut, left.)
2. Grue droite. (Coupé or Cut, right.)
3. Grue gauche.
4. Grue droite.
5. Saut majeur. (Big jump)
6. Posture gauche.

B.
1. Grue droite.
2. Grue gauche.
3. Grue droite.
4. Grue gauche.
5. Saut majeur.
6. Posture droite.

C.
1. Pied croisé droit.
2. Pied croisé droit.
3. Pied croisé gauche.
4. Pied croisé gauche.
5. Saut majeur.
6. Posture droite.

D.
1. Pied croisé gauche.
2. Pied croisé gauche.
3. Pied croisé droit.
4. Pied croisé droit.
5. Saut majeur.
6. Posture gauche.

ALLEMANDE

from Ardern Holt's, *Revived Ancient Dances*

The Allemande is danced as follows, always remembering the intense importance of the head and arm movements; the hands are never loosed, except for a second in changing positions in the third figure:

1. The lady stands in front of the gentleman; he holds her left hand with his left and her right hand with his right. For four bars they go forward and pose, and repeat this four times, the last time they pass forward for two bars only, and turn; this occupies eight bars of the music, and is danced straight across from the left to the right of the stage.

2. Circle four steps round and quick turn; the gentleman turns the lady with arms overhead, and the lady turns the gentleman.

3. Allemande-step forward, change hands quickly, and turn, then allemande-step back slowly, turn and pose.

4. The lady makes four pas de basques in front of the gentleman and turns, the gentleman ending on the right.

5. Four steps across the stage, turn and pose. Take two steps back, turn and pose, and repeat. The Allemande can be danced by one couple or any number of couples placing themselves behind each other. The Allemande step is three pas marchés and the front foot raised.

COURANTE

from Ardern Holt's, *Revived Ancient Dances*

1. Start with a deep curtsey and a springing step forward, and back to fourth position, both arms raised, each dancer turning outwards. These movements occupy four bars of music, and are repeated for another four bars, making eight bars.

2. Eight bars of music are now occupied with a slow pas de basque in a circle, each dancer advancing in an opposite direction, then balancing and turn, making a deep curtsey, and accompanying the steps with arm movements.

3. The dancers spring forward, and each takes one step in an opposite direction to the other, a coupé and half jetté, and this is repeated with the other foot as the dancers turn outwards. They dance the back stay step twice, returning to position and turn, beginning the movement again by repeating the first springing step, and back stay step, so that the partners change places, and turn.

All these three figures are then repeated, commencing with the opposite foot.

SARABANDE

from Playford's *Dancing Master*

1. The dancers stand in two lines. All advance and retire twice, then set to partners, making two steps and closing both feet twice. The first couple on each side join hands and make four steps forward, four back, meet again, and repeat crossing hands, using first the right and then the left hand and repeat, which occupies a phrase of the music played once. The two top dancers on either side join hands and take four steps forward and four back, closing both feet. Then they go round to the right, falling into each other's places; then set with two steps, closing both feet, which occupies the phrase of the music played twice over. This is repeated by all the dancers till none are left.

2. Form into two lines, set to each other. Repeat. The first couple then go down between the second couple. The four then change their places, turn away from each other, and come down to their places. The partners changing places set to each other with two steps, then the feet close together, which occupies two phrases of the music. This is repeated by all taking part.

3. Partners take arms, set with two steps, feet joined together, and turn, this occupying one strain of the music. Repeat, then change places with the second couple on the same side, take right hands across, and go a quarter round. The first couple fall into the places of the second couple. Set and turn, this occupying two phrases of the music. Repeat till all the dancers have carried out the movement.

[119]

MILLER'S JIGG

from Playford's *Dancing Master*

First couple take hands and second couple take hands, then one couple change into the second couple place, and second couple into the first couple place, then back to back with your own and come to your places: the rest do the same. (This to the first part of the time once over.)

The first and second couples take right hands across and go half round, and so go back to back into their own places, then first couple cast off into the second couple place, then all four take hands and go half round, then each man cross over with his own woman and so into their own places again, the other couple do the same. (This to the second strain of the time.)

MENUET DE LA COUR

from Playford's *Dancing Master*

1. The gentleman stands on the left of the lady; each taking a step sideways, so that they face each other; the gentleman, raising his hand, salutes the lady, who curtseys low.
2. Both make a pas marché forward, and facing each other, bow; then turn into their places with another pas marché, and step back.
3. The gentleman, presenting his hand to the lady, leads her forward; they balance to each other with coupé to the right, finishing at opposite corners.
4. Both advance to opposite corners with a pas grave and pas de menuet, finish with right shoulders to each other.
5. Crossing at right angles with the pas marché and minuet step to the corners diagonal to each other, both advance, with a sustained assemblé, ending shoulder to shoulder.
6. Then both back, and turn the contrary shoulder; this they repeat four times, then bending slowly and rising twice.
7. Both raise the arm and join the right hands, making an assemblé; moving round each other, they turn to the right, and finish at opposite corners. 8. Repeat with left hands.
9. They give both hands, and, moving to the right, resume their original places; they then balance, move backward and forward, and finally end with a bow and curtsey.

The minuet step is a demi-coupé with the right foot and one with the left; a pas marché of the right foot on the toes, the legs extended at the end of the step; place the right heel on the ground so that you can bend the knee, and raise the left leg, which passes to the front, making a demi-coupé échapé.

GAVOTTE

to Lully's *Le Ballet du Roi*

The dancers start in a line or circle, one couple separating themselves from the rest. But one couple only can dance it very effectively.

1. Four gavottes forward, four gavottes round, four back, and four round again, the dancers hand in hand, the figure always accompanied by graceful head movements, the partners turning towards each other or apart.

2. Gavotte round the room, the ladies changing sides four times, the dancers hand in hand, but each looking the reverse way and making a step to the side, with the one a curtsey, the other a bow, repeating the step and the reverence.

3. Face partners, taking both hands, and alternate toe and heel step; point toe in front, then behind, then up the room, pivot, and same back, and pivot.

4. Repeat the same step to the right twice, and twice to the left, with partner, four gavottes round.

5. Skate four times; change feet, two pawing steps, gavotte round partner, repeat same step down (two pawing steps) and gavotte round partner.

6. Gavotte forward three times, pirouette back, raise foot up to heel, and advance four times.

Gavotte Step: three steps and an assemblé in 4/4 time. You spring on the foot that is on the ground, and at the same time point the toe of the other foot downwards.

For the half circle round, jump one foot to the side, bringing first the right foot forward and then the left.

BOURREE

from Desrat's *Dictionnaire de la Danse*

STEP in 2/4, on right foot.

    1st beat—pliez left leg, extending right crossed to left at same time; second beat—rise lightly on left leg keeping right extended. (Opposite on left foot.)

BOURREE FROM AUVERGNE—men in one line, women in another.

    1st refrain—

        8 meas.—2 men advance with two opposite women, withdraw, advance again. Ladies and men put hands on hips.

        8 meas.—2 couples at other end do same.

        8 meas.—2 first men advance holding right hands with opposite women, retreat holding left.

        8 meas.—two couples on other end do same.

    2nd refrain—All couples together

    Each man turns with every lady in succession, holding right hands and letting them go under lifted right arm.

    Same figure by women, who turn men under left arm.

    Men and women, hands on hips, bourrée step again forward and back, turn together to return to original places.

RIGAUDON

from Ardern Holt's *Revived Ancient Dances*

Arranged by Isaac, the fashionable dancing master of Queen Anne's court, on the queen's birthday.

Each figure occupies eight bars; both dancers start together without holding hands.

1. Slide and make four running steps, turn, and then pose; repeat with the opposite foot.

2. Turn to left and right alternately four times, going backwards.

3. This figure is danced diagonally to the right with running steps, turn and pose; repeat the same to the left.

4. Two hops and turn, repeat, then run diagonally to the right and turn, run diagonally to the left and turn, with the arms out straight.

5. Half turn to left, half turn to right, whole turn to left, repeat.

6. Arms over head, three steps to left, turn to left, three steps to right, turn to right, hop round and pose with right hand down, the left hand above the head.

7. Balance four times on left foot, four times on right foot, pose as in figure 6.

   The head and arm movements are all important in this dance.

PASSEPIED

from Desrat's *Dictionnaire de la Danse*

Figures—

1. The gentleman and lady cross one foot in front of the other to execute walking steps forward. (Man left in front of right, lady right in front of left.) Opposite couple do same.

2. Each man pirouettes his lady.

3. Couples cross hands to glide to rear. Man describes arc to right, lady to right also. Lady places herself at the man's left to execute this step.

4. Moulinet by all. Ladies in center, gentlemen balance twice.

5. Bow.

6. Pas de basque forward.

7. Form a circle, balance forward and back.

8. 4 men form circle by stretching out arms, ladies circle around own partner to right. Man takes lady's left hand and leads her to her place.

ADDENDA TWO

Suggested Music

PAVANES

1. Luis Milan. (1499-1561) Pavana III. (F major)
2. Pierre Phalese. (1510-1573) Pavane ferrarese. (G minor)
3. Alonso de Mudarra. (15—-15—) Pavana. (A minor)
4. William Byrde. (1540-1623) Pavana. *The Earle of Salisbury.* (A minor)
5. John Bull. (1563-1628) Pavana. *St. Thomas Wake.* (G minor) (The one exception which begins on an up-beat.)
6. Jacques Champion de Chambonnieres. (1620-1670) Pavane. *L'Entretien des Dieux.* (G minor)
7. Jean-Baptiste Lully. (1633-1687) Pavane from *Nopce de Village.* (A minor)
8. Gabriel Faure. (1845-1924) Pavane. op. 50 (F$\sharp$ minor)
9. Maurice Ravel. (1875——) Pavane *de la Belle au bois dormant,* from *Ma Mere l'Oye.* (A minor)
10. Maurice Ravel. (1875——) Pavane *Pour une Infante defunte.* (G major)
11. Walter Niemann. (1876)——)Pavane from *Tafelmusik. op.* 125. (G minor)
12. Francis Poulenc. (1899—) Pavane from *Suite Francaise.* (F major)

GALLIARDS

1. Pierre Phalese. (1510-1573) Galliarde ferrarese. (G minor)
2. William Byrde. (1540-1623) Galiardo. (A minor)
3. John Dowland. (1563-1626) Captaine Digorie Piper, His Galiard. (G minor)

4. John Dowland. (1563-1626) The King of Denmark's Galiard (D minor)

5. Hans Leo Hassler. (1564-1612) Gagliarda. (E minor)

6. Hans Leo Hassler. (1564-1612) Gagliarda. (C. major)

7. Girolamo Frescobaldi.(1583-1644)Gagliarda. (G minor)

8. Girolamo Frescobaldi.(1583-1644)Gagliarda. (D major)

9. Paul Peuerl. (fl. 1602-1625) Galliarde from *Tanzbrevier*. (F major)

10. Bartholomaeus Praetorious. (16—16—) Gagliarda. (E major-A minor) (This is really in A minor but begins and ends with E major chords)

11. Ottorino Respighi. (1879-1935) Gagliarda. Transcribed from Vincenzo Galilei. (1550—) (D major)

ALLEMANDES

1. John Bull. (1563-1628) The Duke of Brunswick's Alman. (A minor)

2. Jean-Baptiste Lully. (1633-1687) Allemande. (E minor)

3. John Blow. (1648-1708) Almand I. (A major)

4. John Blow. (1648-1708) Almand II. (D major)

5. Henry Purcell. (1658-1695) Almand. (G minor)

6. Francois Couperin. (1668-1733) Allemande. *La Tenebreuse*. (C minor)

7. Johann Mattheson. (1681-1764) Allemande. (C minor)

[129]

8. Jean Philippe Rameau. (1683-1764) Allemande. (E minor)

9. Johann Sebastian Bach. (1685-1750) Allemande from *First French Suite*.

10. Georg Friedrich Handel. (1685-1759) Allemande from *Suite XIV*. (G major)

11. Georg Friedrich Handel. (1685-1759) Allemande from *Suite XI*. (D minor)

12. Walter Niemann. (1876—) Allemande from *Tafelmusik*. *op*. 125. (D minor)

SARABANDES

1. Louis Couperin. (1630-1665) Sarabande in Canon Form. (D minor)

2. Francois Couperin. (1668-1733) Sarabande *La Lugubre*. (C minor)

3. Andre Destouches. (1672-1749) Sarabande. (G minor)

4. Jean-Baptiste Loeillet.(1680-1730)Sarabande. (G minor)

5. Jean Phillipe Rameau. (1683-1764) Sarabande from *Zoroastre*. (E major)

6. Georg Friedrich Handel. (1685-1759) Sarabande. (D minor)

7. Claude Debussy. (1862-1918) Sarabande. (C♯ minor)

8. Paul Vidal. (1863-1931) Sarabande from *Zino Zina* (G minor)

9. Erik Satie. (1866-1925) 3 Sarabandes.

10. Arthur Honegger. (1892—) Sarabande (B♭ major)

11. Hermann Reutter. (1900—) Sarabanda, *Christus in Gethsemane.*

12. Henry Brant. (1913—) 2 Sarabandes.

COURANTES

1. Girolamo Frescobaldi. (1583-1644) Corrente. (A minor)

2. Jean-Baptiste Lully. (1633-1687) Courante. (E minor)

3. John Blow. (1648-1708) Corant. (C major)

4. Henry Purcell. (1658-1695) Courant. (G major)

5. Domenico Zipoli. (1675-1726) Corrente. (G minor)

6. Jean-Baptiste Loeillet. (1680-1730) Courante. (G minor)

7. Johann Mattheson. (1681-1764) Courante. (C minor)

8. Georg Friedrich Handel. (1685-1759) Courante. (G major)

9. Johann Kirnberger. (1721-1783) Corrente. (G minor)

10. Walter Niemann (1876—) Courante from *Tafelmusik. op.* 125. (D minor)

11. Cyril Scott. (1879—) Courante. (E minor)

12. Bela Bartok. (1881—) Tre Correnti, transcribed from Michelangelo Rossi. (1630-1660)

COURANTES OF THE 6/4-3/2 VARIETY

13. J. C. de Chambonnieres. (1620-1670) Courante. (A minor)

14. Francois Couperin. (1668-1733) Courante. (G minor)

15. Francois Couperin. (1668-1733) 2 Courantes. (C minor)

16. Francois Couperin. (1668-1733) Courante. (A minor)

17. Francois Couperin. (1668-1733) 2 Courantes. (D minor)

18. Johann Sebastian Bach. (1685-1750) Courante from *Fourth Partita*. (D major)

19. Johann Sebastian Bach. (1685-1750) Courante from *3rd French Suite*. (B minor)

GIGUES

1. Jean-Baptiste Lully. (1633-1687) Gigue. (E minor)

2. John Eccles. (1668-1735). Jigg. (B♭ major)

3. Domenico Zipoli. (1675-1726) Giga. (G minor)

4. Jean-Baptiste Loeillet. (1680-1730) Gigue. (G minor)

5. Jean Philippe Rameau. (1683-1764) 2 Gigues en Rondeau. (E minor-E major)

6. Johann Sebastian Bach. (1685-1750) Gigue from *5th French Suite*. (G major)

7. Georg Friedrich Handel. (1685-1759) Gigue. (D minor)

8. Carl Heinrich Graun. (1701-1759) Gigue. (B♭ minor)

9. Johann P. Kirnberger (1721-1783) Gigue. (C minor)

10. Walter Niemann. (1876—) Gigue from *Tafelmusik, op.* 125. (G major)

11. Alfredo Casella (1883—) Giga from *Pieces enfantines*.

12. Richard Donovan. (1891—) Jig from *Suite for Piano*.

MINUETS

1. Henry Purcell (1658-1695) Minuet. (G major)

2. G. F. Telemann. (1681-1767) Menuett. (A minor)

3. Johann Mattheson. (1681-1764) Menuett. (C minor)

4. J. P. Rameau. (1683-1764) Menuet. (G minor)

5. Gottlied Muffatt. (1683-1770) Minuett. (B♭ major)

6. Johann Sebastian Bach. (1685-1750) Menuet from *6th French Suite*. (E major)

7. J. F. Fasch. (1688-1758) Menuet. (D minor)

8. Erik Satie. (1866-1925) Premier Menuet.

9. Maurice Ravel. (1875—) Menuet from Suite, *Le Tombeau de Couperin*.

10. Walter Niemann. (1876—) Minuet from *Tafelmusik op.* 125. (G major)

11. Alfredo Casella (1883—) Minuetto from *Pieces enfantines*.

12. Serge Prokofieff. (1891)—) Menuetto, op. 32. No. 2.

GAVOTTES

1. Jean-Baptiste Lully. (1633-1687) Gavotte from *L'Amour Malade*. (G minor)
2. Henry Purcell. (1658-1695) Gavotte. (Trumpet Tune called *The Cebell*.) (C major)
3. Louis Marchand. (1669-1732) Gavotte. (D minor)
4. G. P. Telemann. (1681-1767) Gavotte from Overture in A minor.
5. J. P. Rameau. (1683-1764) Gavottes from *Temple de la Gloire*. (D major)
6. Johann Sebastian Bach. (1685-1750) Gavotte from *5th French Suite*. (G major)
7. Johann Sebastian Bach. (1685-1750) Gavotte (with Musette) from *3rd English Suite*. (G minor)
8. Christoph Foerster. (1693-1745) Gavotte. (A major)
9. Arnold Schoenberg. (1874—) Gavotte and Musette from *Suite, op.* 25.
10. Serge Prokofieff. (1891—) Gavotte, op. 12, No. 2. (G minor)
11. Serge Prokofieff. (1891—) Gavotte from *Symphonie Classique, op.* 25. (D major)
12. Serge Prokofieff. (1891—) Gavotta, op. 32, No. 3. (F♯ minor)

BOURREES

1. J.-B. Lully. (1633-1687) Bourrée from *Phaeton*. (C major)
2. Johann Kuhnau. (1677-1722) Bourrée. (D minor)

3. G. P. Telemann. (1681-1767) Bourrée. (A minor)

4. Jean Joseph Mouret. (1682-1738) Bourrée from *Les Amours de Ragonde*. (E major)

5. Johann Sebastian Bach. (1685-1750) Bourrée from *2nd Violin Sonata*. (B minor)

6. G. F. Handel. (1685-1759) Bourrée. (G minor)

7. J. F. Fasch. (1688-1758) Bourrée. (B♭ major)

8. Gottfried Heinrich Stölzel. (1690-1749) Bourrée. (G minor)

9. J. L. Krebs. (1713-1780) Bourrée II. (A major)

10. J. P. Kirnberger. (1721-1783) Bourrée. (D major)

11. Aime Lachaume. (1871—) Gavotte-Bourrée from *Trianon Suite*. (G minor)

RIGAUDONS

1. Henry Purcell. (1658-1695) Riggadoon. (C major)
2. Francois Couperin. (1668-1733) Rigaudon. (D minor)
3. John Barrett. (1674-1735) Rigadoon. *The St. Catherine*. (A major)
4. J. P. Rameau. (1683-1764) Rigaudon. (E minor)
5. J. P. Rameau. (1683-1764) Rigaudon from *Dardanus*. (G major)
6. J. P. Kirnberger. (1721-1783) Rigaudon. (D major)
7. Edward MacDowell. (1861-1908) Rigaudon. op. 49, No. 2. (A major)

8. Dalhousie Young. (1866-1921) Rigaudon. *Sailors' Hornpipe.* (D minor)

9. Percy Pitt. (1870-1932) Rigodon. (C major)

10. Walter Niemann. (1876—) Rigaudon from *Tafelmusik, op.* 125. (D major)

11. Walter Niemann. (1876—) Rigaudon. op. 5, No. 5. (G major)

12. Serge Prokofieff. (1891—) Rigaudon. op. 12, No. 3. (C major)

PASSEPIEDS

1. André Campra. (1660-1744) Passepieds from *L'Europe Galante.* (G major)

2. Fr. Couperin. (1668-1733) Passepied. (D minor)

3. Andre Destouches. (1672-1749) Passepieds *en Rondeau* from *Issé.* (G minor)

4. Gottfried Grünewald. (1675-1739) Passepied. (G major)

5. G. P. Telemann. (1681-1767) Passepied. (A major)

6. J. P. Rameau. (1683-1764) Passepieds from *Castor et Pollux.* (E major)

7. Johann Sebastian Bach. (1685-1750) Passepied from *5th English Suite.* (E minor)

8. Johann Sebastian Bach. (1685-1750) Passepied from *5th Partita.* (G major)

9. G. F. Handel. (1685-1759) Passepied from *Aylesford Pieces.* (G major)

10. Chr. Foerster. (1693-1745) Passepied. (A major)

11. J. P. Kirnberger. (1721-1783) Passepied. (E major)

12. Percy Turnbull. (pub. 1925) Passepied. (A major)

CHACONNES AND PASSACAGLIAS

1. J. H. d'Anglebert. (1628-1691) Chaconne. (D major)

2. Louis Couperin. (1630-1665) Chaconne. (G minor)

3. Johann Pachelbel. (1653-1706) Ciaconna. (D major)

4. Johann Pachelbel. (1653-1706) Ciaccona. (F minor)

5. Johann Pachelbel. (1653-1706) Passacaglia. (D minor)

6. Henry Purcell. (1658-1695) Chaconne. (F major)

7. Francois Couperin. (1668-1733) Chaconne-Rondeau. (C minor)

8. Francois Couperin. (1668-1733) Passacaille. (B minor)

9. G. F. Handel. (1685-1759) Chaconne with 9 Variations. (G major)

10. G. F. Handel. (1685-1759) Chaconne with 62 Variations. (G major)

11. E. R. Blanchet. (1877—) Passacaglia. *Tocsin.*

12. Arnold Bax. (1883—) Passacaglia. *Paean.*

Index

[139]

47 50

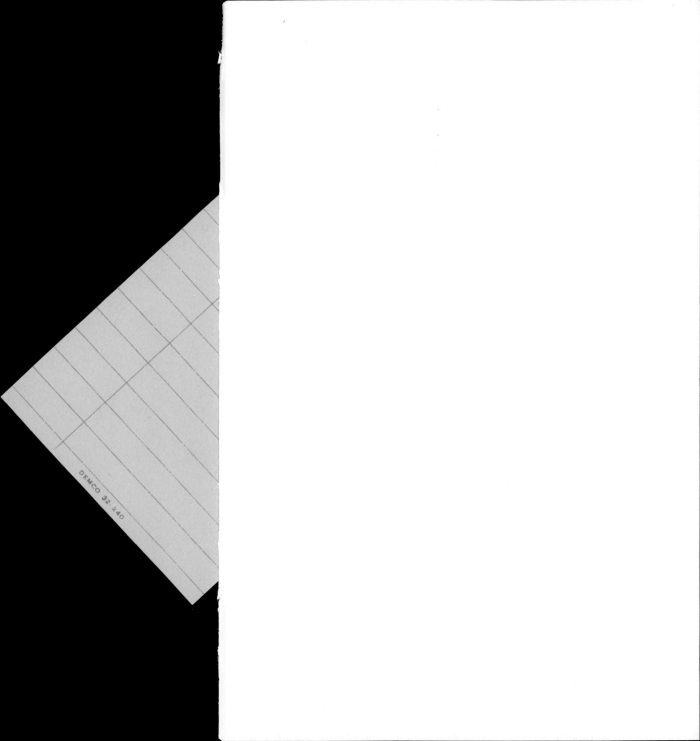

DEMCO 32 240

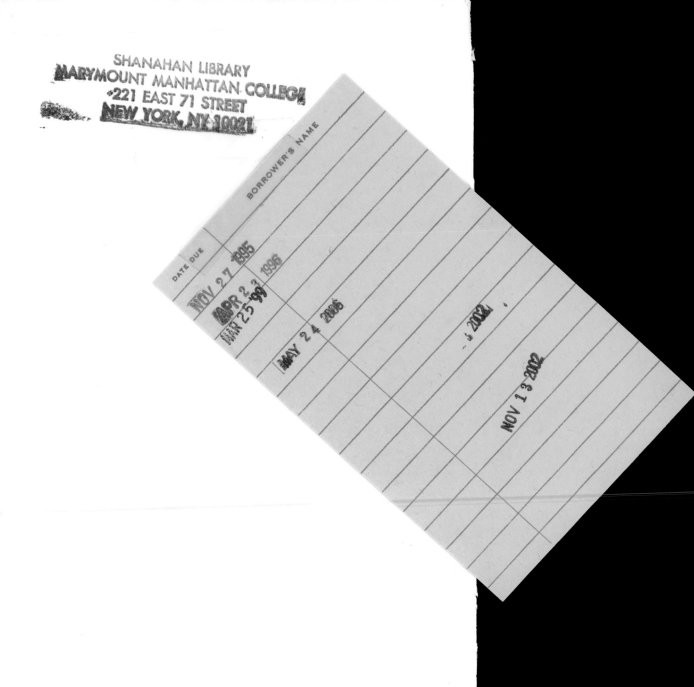